Reading
God's Word
Today

Reading
God's Word
Today

A Practical and Faith-filled Approach to Scripture

George Martin

Our Sunday Visitor Publishing Division
Our Sunday Visitor, Inc.
Huntington, Indiana 46750

For Bert and Mary Lou Ghezzi

Scripture texts in this work are taken from the *New American Bible with Revised New Testament and Revised Psalms* © 1991, 1986, 1970 Confraternity of Christian Doctrine, Washington, D.C. and are used by permission of the copyright owner. All Rights Reserved. No part of the *New American Bible* may be reproduced in any form without permission in writing from the copyright owner.

Every reasonable effort has been made to determine copyright holders of excerpted materials and to secure permissions as needed. If any copyrighted materials have been inadvertently used in this work without proper credit being given in one form or another, please notify Our Sunday Visitor in writing so that future printings of this work may be corrected accordingly.

Our Sunday Visitor Publishing Division
Our Sunday Visitor, Inc.
200 Noll Plaza
Huntington, IN 46750
1-800-348-2440
bookpermissions@osv.com

ISBN: 978-1-59276-640-6 (Inventory No. T922)
LCCN: 2009934462

Cover design by Rebecca J. Heaston / Cover image: Shutterstock
Interior design by Sherri L. Hoffman

PRINTED IN THE UNITED STATES OF AMERICA

Contents

Preface

The Purpose of This Book

This book is about reading Scripture as God's word addressed to us.

It is a practical book, intended to help those who wish to begin reading Scripture or want to mature in their understanding of Scripture. It focuses on the way that God addresses his word to us through the words of Scripture and on our using Scripture to grow in our relationship with God.

I began writing the predecessor of this book in 1972, convinced that a book like it was needed. I had worked in Catholic adult education, organizing Scripture classes along with other programs. Finding textbooks for Scripture courses was a challenge, for there weren't nearly as many good books on the Bible back then as there are now. Those that were available explained the Bible, but they did not explain how one ought to go about reading the Bible.

Yet that was the help most of the adults who enrolled in Scripture courses needed. Like many Catholics, they had grown up not reading the Bible. Now, in the wake of the Second Vatican Council, they wanted to start but didn't know where to begin: *What translation should I use? How should I apply the message of the Bible to my life? What do I do when I come across a passage I don't understand?* Introductions to Scripture and commentaries on its books did not address such questions. Many still have such questions today.

I had started reading Scripture on a daily basis some years earlier. Through the grace of God and some pointers I picked up from others,* I developed an approach to Scripture that worked well for me. I decided to write a book that would help others read Scripture as God's word. The book that resulted, the first edition of *Reading Scripture as the Word of God*, helped a number of people get off on the right foot in reading the Bible, if I can judge from the letters and comments I received.

The book was periodically revised through the years as it went through four editions. The time arrived, however, to thoroughly rework its contents, dropping material that did not address today's needs and adding new material and resources that did, and revising throughout. The reworking was so extensive that it was appropriate to publish the resulting book under a new title: *Reading God's Word Today*. The aim of the new presentation remains the same as that of its predecessor: to provide practical help for reading Scripture as God's word to us.

Part I of this book is on Reading Scripture. It provides practical suggestions for reading Scripture, for growing in understanding what we read, for listening to the word of God speak to us through Scripture, and for using Scripture in our prayer. Its purpose is to help Scripture "come alive" for us.

Part II is on The Word of God and is concerned with how God reveals himself to us through the words of Scripture. It discusses how we should approach Scripture as the word of God spoken to us in human words, and how Scripture reveals God to us, forming us into his people. It also offers a few pointers for our ongoing reading of God's word.

To simplify this book, references to sources are usually made in abbreviated form, with complete information provided at the end of the book.

---

*Although I will forgo further footnotes in this book, I need to acknowledge that I was particularly helped by a sermon of Søren Kierkegaard, "What is required to look at oneself with true blessing in the mirror of the word?" found in *For Self-Examination* (Minneapolis: Augsburg, 1963), and by a booklet by Pius Parsch, *Learning to Read the Bible* (Collegeville, MN: The Liturgical Press, 1963).

Each chapter includes a short list of recommended resources designed to help you read, understand, and pray Scripture as God's word.

A Study Guide consisting of questions is found at the end of each chapter. The questions can stimulate personal reflection and provide a basis for small group sharing. For both individuals and groups, I recommend reading the Bible itself right from the start, rather than waiting until one finishes this book. Members of a group could decide to read the same book of the Bible in order to focus their sharing. Alternatively, it could be left up to each member of the group to decide where to begin reading, so that a greater variety of experiences could be shared.

PART I

Reading Scripture

ONE

Reading

For just as from the heavens
the rain and snow come down
And do not return there
till they have watered the earth,
making it fertile and fruitful,
Giving seed to him who sows
and bread to him who eats,
So shall my word be
that goes forth from my mouth;
It shall not return to me void,
but shall do my will,
achieving the end for which I sent it.

— Is 55:10-11

God's word broke into the life of Abram over three thousand years ago, beginning a stream of revelation that reached its fulfillment in Jesus Christ and continues for us today.

God's word bid Abram to leave his country and father's house for a new land (Gen 12:1-3). Abram's willing response changed his life and changed human history: Abram became Abraham, the father of a people that God adopted as his own. Through this people, God continued to speak his word, revealing himself to humankind.

In the fullness of time, God's word came not merely as a message but as a person: the Word of God became flesh and lived in our midst (Jn 1:14). God's Word was not only spoken to us but became one of us, Jesus of Nazareth.

Today we can drink from that same stream of revelation. God reveals himself to us, God adopts us as daughters and sons, God gives us life itself, through his Word spoken to us, Jesus Christ.

God sends his word to us as he sent it to Abram: to reveal himself, to transform us, to create for himself a people. His word is not an empty or powerless word; it is a life-giving word, a transforming word.

The word of God is spoken to us in a variety of ways. It is spoken through the Church. It is spoken to our hearts in prayer. And it is spoken through the words of the Bible. Listening to the word of God spoken to us through the words of Scripture can transform us, drawing us into a closer relationship with God. Scripture can be a means for God to take hold of us and reshape us, bringing us to fuller life. Scripture speaks of the power of God's word. "Is not my word like fire, says the Lord, / like a hammer shattering rocks?" (Jer 23:29). "Indeed, the word of God is living and effective, sharper than any two-edged sword, penetrating even between soul and spirit, joints and marrow, and able to discern reflections and thoughts of the heart" (Heb 4:12).

> God sends his word to us as he sent it to Abram: to reveal himself, to transform us, to create for himself a people.

This powerful word of God is addressed to us.

This book is about reading Scripture as the word of God, about reading it in such a way that God can speak his word to us and transform us. This book is about listening to the word of God and embracing it, so that his word does not return to him empty but carries out his will within us.

Daily Reading

The first step in listening to the word of God speak to us through Scripture is to begin reading the Bible and read it *daily.*

Some begin to read Scripture with a jackrabbit start, a resolution to read the Bible from cover to cover — but then wear down and fail to carry out their resolve. The Bible is a big book (it is a library, in fact), too big to be read simply in a burst of enthusiasm. If we are ever to read it thoroughly, our reading must be sustained by commitment rather than enthusiasm. If we are to become immersed in its revelation to us, our reading must become an integral part of our lives, not just an incidental activity that we do now and then.

The most practical step we can take to read the Bible as God's word to us is to commit ourselves to reading it every day. Our reading need not take a lot of time; fifteen minutes is an acceptable commitment. But it must be done faithfully, day after day, no matter how we feel or how hectic things are for us. This kind of faithfulness requires a firm determination to read the Bible fifteen minutes every day, no matter what.

Why do I recommend fifteen minutes a day for our basic reading? Five minutes is too little to really immerse oneself in the word of God; a half an hour is too long for most of us to sustain an alert and prayerful reading of Scripture, at least at the beginning. Of course, if you are receiving special graces from God drawing you to a deep reading of Scripture for a longer period, by all means do so.

> The sacred synod also earnestly and especially urges all the Christian faithful, especially Religious, to learn by frequent reading of the divine Scriptures the "excellent knowledge of Jesus Christ" (Phil 3:8). "For ignorance of the Scriptures is ignorance of Christ" (St. Jerome). Therefore, they should gladly put themselves in touch with the sacred text itself, whether it be through the liturgy, rich in the divine word, or through devotional reading, or through

instructions suitable for the purpose and other aids which, in our time, with approval and active support of the shepherds of the Church, are commendably spread everywhere.

— VATICAN II, *DIVINE REVELATION*, NO. 25

Daily reading is the foundation for reading Scripture as the word of God. Of course, daily reading isn't sufficient in itself. Our reading should be done prayerfully and our understanding of Scripture must be aided by study, making use of the various helps at our disposal. Further, we need some understanding of the role that Scripture plays in God's revelation of himself, and some skill in listening to God speak to us through the words of Scripture. But all our skills in understanding the Bible must begin and end in our actually reading the Bible, so that our lives may be transformed by him who speaks to us through its words.

This vital reading of Scripture should be part of our daily spiritual nourishment and routine. Reading Scripture isn't like going out to dinner on special occasions; it must be like the evening supper that families share, day in, day out. Periodic times of intensive reading of the Bible are a good idea, just as occasional evenings out together build a marriage. But just as our daily supper nourishes us, our daily reading of Scripture will bring the strength of God into our lives. Anything less may lead to spiritual malnutrition.

The process of our growth into the image of Christ begins with our baptism into Jesus Christ and will end with the resurrection of our bodies into everlasting union with him. Throughout, God continually calls us to grow in love and discipleship. At all times we must listen to the word of God speaking to us, beckoning us on. Our need to read Scripture to listen to God's voice never ends.

The complexity of Scripture and its inexhaustible depths shouldn't discourage us from beginning to read it. We aren't called to read the Bible in order to pass a test at the end of the month, or at the end of a year. The "test" will come at the end of our lives, and then we shall be asked about our love, not about our ability as Scripture scholars. God has given us Scripture precisely to help us meet this test of love. We must not be overwhelmed by what we do not know about Scripture; we should be consoled that God has given us Scripture as a means of growing in faith, in hope, in love, in union with him.

We aren't called to read the Bible in order to pass a test at the end of the month, or at the end of a year. The "test" will come at the end of our lives, and then we shall be asked about our love, not about our ability as Scripture scholars.

We shall grow in union with God as we begin a program of daily reading of Scripture and pursue this program faithfully. We can underestimate the impact of a modest commitment, honored day after day, year after year. The fruit of our Scripture reading is something that is better experienced than described.

We marvel at the beauty of the Grand Canyon — a wonder created by the Colorado River's slow but persistent erosion, an erosion too slow to be seen except in its fantastic effects.

Something similar can happen in us. We have 1440 minutes to live each day of our lives. If we spend fifteen of those minutes prayerfully listening to the word of God speak to us through the words of Scripture, it will make a difference in the other 1425 minutes. If we spend a few minutes alone with God's word every day, in the course of our years, they will play a significant role in our transformation in Christ.

The Bible is not a book of magic; by itself it cannot change our lives, no matter how much we read it. It can, however, be a means whereby the same Holy Spirit who inspired the authors of the Bible can inspire us — and not only inspire us to understand what we read, but empower us to enter into the reality that we read about. What is sacred for us about sacred Scripture is that through the words of Scripture, we can listen to the words of

God; through listening to and embracing the words of God, we can be transformed into his image.

The Bible is not a book to be learned and mastered, like a book of ancient history. Nor is it like a detective novel that we can read once to find out "whodunit" and set it aside. It is a book that we need to return to each day, rereading familiar passages in order to enter more deeply into the mystery that they reveal.

To enter into this mystery of God's word, your lifetime of listening to the word of God can begin *today* with a fifteen-minute reading. Stop reading this book fifteen minutes sooner than you had planned and begin reading the Gospel according to Luke. Then continue reading Scripture daily for the rest of your life.

Reading the Bible every day isn't sufficient in itself. We must approach our reading in a certain way; we need practical help with Scripture's complexities; we need to embrace God's word as we hear it. The rest of this book discusses these and other matters. But we must first read, daily and faithfully. Begin today, and continue tomorrow, and the day after that.

Kinds of Reading

There are various kinds of Scripture reading, each having its own pace and characteristics.

Sometimes, we may quickly read through a whole book or long section of Scripture to get an overview of it. It is profitable, for instance, to read some of Paul's shorter letters as we would read any letter we receive: reading it through from beginning to end, and then going back through it more slowly a second time. This type of reading is also appropriate for many parts of the Old Testament, particularly the historical books. A straight-through reading of a long section provides an idea of "the lay of the land"; the more significant passages can be marked for later careful reading and reflection.

At the other end of the scale lies prolonged meditation on a single verse or a few verses from Scripture. Here, the object is not to cover ground or read new material, but to understand as fully as possible a single thought, and to reflect on its applications to one's own life. There are many verses in Scripture whose meaning we will not exhaust in a lifetime of reflection.

Between the sustained reading of a long passage (or entire books of Scripture) and intensive attention to a few words lies the kind of reading that should form the basis of our daily reading of Scripture. Our fifteen-minute reading should be a reflective and prayerful reading, alert to both context and detail. This kind of reading is characterized neither by a desire to cover a certain amount of material, nor by an attempt to milk the last ounce of meaning from every single verse. It is careful reading, with pauses to reflect on the meaning of what is being read. It is slow reading, leisurely reading, with attention to nuance. It is reading at a deliberate yet natural pace that allows us to linger over a single verse or thought before continuing on.

> Careful daily reading is the foundation of our listening to the word of God speak to us through Scripture, including when it is proclaimed in the liturgy.

Each type of reading has its usefulness. Careful daily reading is the foundation of our listening to the word of God speak to us through Scripture, including when it is proclaimed in the liturgy. The more rapid reading of whole books should be a part of our Scripture study, and meditation on a few words or verses a part of our daily prayer.

Our reading of Scripture should be done in such a way that the words sink in, that we grasp the meaning not only with our heads, but also with our hearts. This type of reading can be compared to gazing at a great painting, or to reading poetry. The point in looking at a painting is not to give it a quick glance, say, "That's a painting of a woman," and pass on. Art must be viewed contemplatively, with attention both to the broad sweeps of color and design, and to the details. So, too, with reading a poem: poetry is not meant for speed reading, or to be read once and discarded. Poetry is meant to be read slowly and savored, and to be read repeatedly.

God's word must also be read slowly and savored. We need to understand the broad sweep of the passage we are reading — an event in Jesus' life, an argument from Paul, a prophecy from Isaiah. But we also need to be alert to the details, the nuances of meaning. Even the shortest verse in the Bible has depths of meaning: "And Jesus wept" (Jn 11:35).

> Above all, we need to ask, "What is the author trying to tell the reader?"

Above all, we need to ask, "What is the author trying to tell the reader?" "Why did Luke think it important to include this event from the life of Jesus?" "What is Paul trying to get across to the Corinthians?" "What is the point of this prophecy of Isaiah?" This demands that we think about what we are reading as we are reading it; this requires that we read slowly. Our reading should be paced by our understanding, not by our watches.

Practical Considerations

Some problems may emerge as soon as we resolve to spend fifteen minutes a day reading Scripture. First, and perhaps most urgently, how do we find the time in our busy schedules? Second, which of the many translations of the Bible should we choose for our reading? Finally, where do we begin? These problems will not afflict everyone equally. Some people's schedules are busier than others; many have long since decided on a favorite translation of the Bible; many have already begun daily reading. Nevertheless, these practical issues need to be addressed.

Finding *the* Time

The most common obstacle to daily Scripture reading is not finding the time, but finding *the* time. We all have plenty of time — in the sense that none of us have lives so fully scheduled that we don't have at least fifteen free minutes each day. However, many have trouble finding *the right* fifteen minutes to be alone with God and his word.

Some people wake up too groggy in the morning to undertake anything as important as reading God's word. But by noon, the cares of the day have descended in force, and distractions pile on distractions. In the evening, fatigue may seem to prohibit anything more strenuous than passively watching television.

> The most common obstacle to daily Scripture reading is not finding the time, but finding *the* time.

I suspect that most of us could come up with a list of reasons why there is no suitable period at any time in our day for reading Scripture. Perhaps the thing to do is to make such a list, and then *pick a definite time anyway.* We can admit that no time is perfect but firmly resolve to set aside fifteen minutes, regardless — the least worst time if no time is perfect.

For those who wake up alert, the first minutes in the morning may be the most peaceful and distraction-free time of the day. Don't think about all the things that have to be done that day. Simply turn to the Lord, and then turn to your bookmark in the Bible and begin reading.

Others may find the quiet of the evening an ideal time to place themselves in the presence of the Lord and listen to his word. After the day's work is done we may have the freedom to turn wholeheartedly to God and listen to him without distraction.

Still others will find other times during their days when fifteen minutes can be set aside. It may be at the kitchen table after children go to school; it may be at one's desk during the first minutes of lunch hour; it may be a visit to a nearby church. *Everyone* can find the time.

What is important is that we make the time, and that it be a time when our minds are sufficiently alert and free to use the time profitably. For most of us, a vague resolve to spend fifteen minutes "sometime during the day" reading Scripture is unrealistic: sometimes we will, and sometimes we won't. To prevent that haphazard approach, we need to set a definite time each day.

Choosing a Translation

To read Scripture with understanding, we need a good translation — perhaps even several good translations, since no translation is perfect.

The first requirement for a translation is accuracy: the faithful rendering of the meaning of the Hebrew, Aramaic, and Greek in which the books of Scripture were written. The second requirement is that the meaning of the original be conveyed in fluent English. Fulfilling both requirements is no small task; many modern translations are the product of committees of scholars and years of work.

It is hard to detect much difference in modern translations of Scripture based on church denominations. We are at the end of the era when Catholic and Protestant translations vied with each other. The translations being done today are generally based on a scholarship that cuts across denominational lines. Certain translations may be labeled "Catholic" or "Protestant" largely on the basis of whether they include or omit those books of the Old Testament which Catholics hold to be a part of Scripture but which Protestants consider "Apocryphal." However, some "Protestant" translations are available in editions that include all the books Catholics consider to be inspired.

> To read Scripture with understanding, we need a good translation — perhaps even several good translations, since no translation is perfect.

I suggest three translations for your consideration:

- The *New American Bible* was translated by members of the Catholic Biblical Association of America and first published in 1970. Since then it has gone through successive stages of revision. This translation is both accurate and readable, and reflects the latest scholarship. Introductions to each of the books of Scripture and footnotes are also done by members of the Catholic Biblical Association. The *New American Bible* translation is the basis of the lectionary readings used in the liturgy of the Catholic Church in America. Reader's surveys I carried out when I was the editor of *God's Word Today* magazine revealed that the *New American Bible* was by far the most popular translation for subscribers. Scripture quotations in this book are drawn from it.

• The *Jerusalem Bible* appeared in English in 1966, based on a French counterpart completed ten years earlier by scholars at the École Biblique in Jerusalem — a venerable Catholic biblical institute under the direction of French Dominicans. A thoroughly revised translation appeared as the *New Jerusalem Bible* in 1991, based on a second edition of the French counterpart. The *New Jerusalem Bible* is a translation from the original languages, but made with an eye to the interpretations of the French translators. The introductions to the various books and the notes are basically translations of the introductions and notes from the French edition.

• The *Revised Standard Version* was made by Protestant scholars and published in 1952. It is a revision of the earlier American Standard and King James versions, but a revision in light of the Hebrew, Aramaic, and Greek manuscripts. The *Revised Standard Version*, seeking to preserve its literary heritage from the earlier translations, is usually characterized as both a literal and a literate translation. It was published in an updated form as the *New Revised Standard Version* in 1989 and is widely used. It is available in various Catholic editions that include the Old Testament books that Catholics call "Deuterocanonical" and Protestants call "Apocryphal."

Although the *New American Bible*, the *New Jerusalem Bible*, and the *New Revised Standard Version* can each be faulted for certain lapses or infelicities, the same can be said of every translation. These three translations may be used as reliable translations into understandable English.

There are many other translations/versions of Scripture available:

The *Living Bible* is more a paraphrase than a literal translation; thus, despite its readability, I don't recommend it. I believe it's better to wrestle with the difficulties of a more literal translation of Scripture than rely on a paraphrase of what the inspired authors wrote.

Two other translations are venerable, but dated: the Catholic Douay-Rheims and the Protestant King James Version, both made in the seventeenth century. Scripture scholarship has made significant advances in the centuries since they appeared, and modern translations are based on a more accurate Hebrew, Aramaic, and Greek texts of Scripture than were available three hundred years ago. Equally important, the English language has changed since the Douay-Rheims and King James translations were made, with many words having different meanings today. Consequently, I don't recommend use of the Douay-Rheims and King James translations.

> There is value in consistently reading one translation of Scripture and allowing its phrasing of key passages to become familiar, almost to the point of unconscious memorization.

There is value in consistently reading one translation of Scripture and allowing its phrasing of key passages to become familiar, almost to the point of unconscious memorization. An important part of our understanding of Scripture comes when we read one passage but hear echoes of others — for example, when we sense a Gospel reference to the Servant Songs of Isaiah without having to check references in the footnotes. To have read and reread and meditated on one translation allows its phrasing and cadences to sink into our minds.

At the same time, other translations will bring out different nuances in familiar passages, and provide us with fresh insights. No one translation can fully capture the riches and beauty of Scripture. It can be helpful to consult different translations in order to better grasp the meaning of a passage. This is particularly true when we are studying an important passage of Scripture and meditating on its significance for us. While we might rely mainly on one translation of Scripture, a second and perhaps even a third translation can be kept at hand and referred to in the course of our study.

> I recommend making an investment in a high-quality edition of the Bible, complete with notes and introductions, and buying a second translation (at least of the New Testament) for comparative purposes.

I recommend making an investment in a high-quality edition of the Bible, complete with notes and introductions, and buying a second translation (at least of the New Testament) for comparative purposes.

Finally, we shouldn't hope for *the* perfect translation, *the* unambiguous rendering of every passage, *the* undisputed meaning of every text. No translation is perfect; no translation is sacred — even of sacred Scripture. A phrase or idiom from another language often may be translated in more than one way. Scholars have been translating the Scriptures since Jews in Alexandria, Egypt, began to put the Hebrew Scriptures into Greek, around 200 B.C. New translations will undoubtedly continue to appear, each trying to better render the languages of Scripture into our own.

Where to Begin

For someone approaching the Bible for the first time, it would be a bad idea to begin with the first verse of the first chapter of the book of Genesis, and plan on reading the Bible straight through to the last verse of the last chapter of the book of Revelation. Contrary to what some might expect, the books of the Bible don't appear in the order they were written, nor even in the historical order of the events they describe. There is no particular advantage to beginning our Scripture reading with Genesis, and several disadvantages. Most likely we will bog down somewhere in the laws of Leviticus or the genealogies of Numbers, get discouraged, and abandon our reading.

Rather, since we read Scripture as followers of Christ and members of his Church, I recommend reading first the two works by Luke in the New Testament: the Gospel according to Luke and the Acts of the Apostles. These two books of the New Testament are a two-volume work in themselves, telling us of the good news of Jesus Christ and of how it was proclaimed "to the ends of the earth" (Acts 1:8).

Alternately, the Gospel according to Mark could provide a good beginning point, with Paul's letters to the Thessalonians and Corinthians the second stage. John's Gospel stands at the summit of New Testament revelation, but requires very meditative reading. Paul's letters to the Romans and Galatians present his most profound reflections on the mystery of redemption through Jesus Christ, and demand careful study. The book of Revelation should probably be the last book of the New Testament to be approached. It cannot be simply read; it must be studied with the help of a suitable commentary or other aid if it is to be understood.

The vastness of the Old Testament should not inhibit us. Selective reading is more appropriate here: lists of genealogies and pages of dietary laws may well be skimmed on first reading. The first five books of the Old Testament lay out God's covenant with his people. The historical books (especially Joshua, Judges, Samuel, and Kings) provide the background for understanding the books of the prophets. And the prophets in turn provide background necessary for understanding the Gospels. The other books of the Old Testament contain wisdom, proverbs, prayers, and national stories of the Israelites.

In reading the Old Testament, some kind of study aid is almost essential. Using an edition of the Bible with good introductions and notes for the various books of Scripture can make a big difference. I will say more about growing in our understanding of Scripture and using study aids in the next chapter.

In addition to reading the Bible book by book, some follow the Scripture readings in the lectionary used in the liturgy — two readings on most weekdays, and three readings on Sunday. Reflecting on one or more of the lectionary readings before going to church helps us to understand and take to heart the readings as they are proclaimed to us during the liturgy. I don't recommend, however, making the lectionary readings our only reading of Scripture. Not all of the Bible can be fitted into the lectionary, so much is left out. Some lectionary readings (particularly from the Old Testament) are difficult to understand outside of their context in the book in which they occur. Reading the Bible book by book provides us with the background necessary for understanding the lectionary readings.

> Reflecting on one or more of the lectionary readings before going to church helps us to understand and take to heart the readings as they are proclaimed to us during the liturgy.

Prayer before Reading

The most important preparation for reading Scripture as the word of God is prefacing our reading with prayer. It need not be lengthy prayer, but we do need to turn our hearts and minds to God. Our reading of Scripture is not reading for the sake of reading; it is reading for the sake of listening to him who speaks to us through Scripture.

We can best begin that listening by turning to God, much as we turn toward another person who is talking to us. When we converse with someone, we need to pay attention to her or him, and not to whatever else may be going on around us. It is impolite — as well as distracting — to try to watch television or read the newspaper while carrying on a conversation. So, too, with our reading of Scripture: we should first turn our attention to God, whom we wish to hear. We should tune out all else, not for the sake of "rejecting the world" but simply as a matter of expediency: we can do only one thing well at a time.

A simple act of turning our minds and hearts to God is the beginning of all prayer, and must likewise be the beginning of our reading Scripture as the word of God. If we are particularly distracted by cares and concerns, we may have to sit quietly for a few minutes, relax, and put distractions out of our minds. It is a proper and necessary thing to take our cares and concerns to the Lord in prayer — but not in a way that prevents us from praying, or from listening to him.

> A simple act of turning our minds and hearts to God is the beginning of all prayer, and must likewise be the beginning of our reading Scripture as the word of God.

Sometimes, it is helpful to hold our Bible in our hands for a moment before opening it and remind ourselves that this book contains God's word to us: "I am about to read Scripture. I am about to read God's word to me. I want to pay full attention to what I read. I want to accept the word that I read and try to make it a part of my life."

Our prayer before reading should ask two things of God. First, we should pray that the same Holy Spirit who guided the writing of Scripture will be present in us, inspiring us to correctly understand what we read, and to understand it in ever-increasing depth. We can apply the words of the Second Vatican Council to our reading of Scripture: "The interior help of the Holy Spirit must precede and assist, moving the heart and turning it to God, opening the eyes of the mind and giving joy and ease in assenting to the truth and believing it."

— DIVINE REVELATION, NO. 5

Second, our prayer should ask that we will be empowered to make what we read a part of our lives. We must be "doers of the word and not hearers only" (Jas 1:22). Embracing and living by what we read, as well as understanding it, requires the power of the Holy Spirit in us — and so, too, it should be a matter of our prayer.

If we fully understand what we are praying, we can pray simply, "Lord, speak to me." These simple words can express our turning our minds and hearts to him, our eagerness to understand his word through the presence of his Spirit within us, and our resolve to be formed by his word, conforming our lives to what he asks and offers.

We could also make the prayer of Samuel our prayer: "Speak, LORD, for your servant is listening" (1 Sam 3:9). It isn't so much the words we say as the attitude of heart we have in saying them.

We do not approach the Bible as we approach any other book; we approach it as an opportunity to listen to him who speaks to us through the words of Scripture. We approach God himself, and our attitude must be one of prayer.

> The obedience of faith (Rom 13:26; see 1:5; 2 Cor 10:5-6) is to be given to God who reveals . . . To make this act of faith, the grace of God and the interior help of the Holy Spirit must precede and assist, moving the heart and turning it to God, opening the eyes of the mind and giving joy and ease to everyone in assenting to the truth and believing it. To bring about an ever deeper understanding of revelation the same Holy Spirit constantly brings faith to completion by His gifts.
>
> — DIVINE REVELATION, NO. 5

Faithfulness and Humility

It is easy to resolve to read the Bible daily; it can be a challenge to remain faithful to our resolution. Some days, we may fall into bed at night without having read Scripture that day, despite our intention to do so. We may be tempted to think that we will never be very faithful to daily Scripture reading.

What should we do when we fail and are tempted to give up trying? One answer lies in choosing the best time that is available to us, and safeguarding it as best we can. But equally important can be our attitude toward achieving daily Scripture reading, and the way we cope with our failures to do so.

> So he said to Samuel, "Go to sleep, and if you are called, reply, 'Speak, LORD, for your servant is listening.'" When Samuel went to sleep in his place, the LORD came and revealed his presence, calling out as before, "Samuel, Samuel!" Samuel answered, "Speak, for your servant is listening."
>
> — 1 SAM 3:9-10

Many of us quit too easily. We fall, and pick ourselves up, and fall again. After four or five falls, we give up the struggle, thinking that we are doomed to fail forever. Rather than strain after an ideal that continually seems to elude us, we lower our expectations of ourselves until they match where we are. If we haven't been able to make daily Scripture reading a part of our lives after a few weeks or months, we assume we will never be able to do so and give up the effort.

In my own life, I find that change comes exceedingly slowly and gradually. I don't know that I have ever been able to change myself or my behavior immediately, simply because I decided that it was right to do so. Whatever changes or growth have taken place in me have come only after sustained effort and prayer.

To make daily Scripture reading a part of our lives may take a sustained effort. If we are committed to staying with our resolve, no matter how often we fail, then we can be a little more patient with ourselves when we do fail. We didn't expect to remake ourselves instantly, and sure enough, we haven't. But we are still trying, and with God's grace we will succeed.

We may have good days and bad days in reading Scripture, as in everything else we do. Some days, the print will seem to leap off the page at us, full of meaning for our lives. Reading Scripture is then a pure joy, and we may have trouble tearing ourselves away from it. Yet at other times not only will the print fail to leap off the page, but it will seem to blur before our eyes. Our reading can be decidedly dry, uninspiring, and burdensome. Our minds will wander despite our best effort to concentrate, and we may be very tempted to give up the whole enterprise.

> It would be unwise to give up reading Scripture because it seems to be dry and unrewarding. We can learn much, and profit greatly, even on those days when nothing seems to be happening as we read.

We should hope and pray to receive the grace of Scripture coming alive for us. And there are ways of reading that can help in making it come alive; some of these will be discussed in Chapter Three. But it would be unwise to give up reading Scripture because it seems to be dry and unrewarding. We can learn much, and profit greatly, even on those days when nothing seems to be happening as we read. As in the rest of the Christian life, "in due time we shall reap our harvest, if we do not give up" (Gal 6:9). If athletes only worked out when they felt like it, they would never get in good enough shape to win. They would never even get in good enough shape to ever enjoy working out.

Sometimes, our problems of dryness may stem from a seeming over-familiarity with a given passage. We can read the first few words of a familiar parable, and find that our minds jump through the entire parable to the end. Our eyes may continue reading, but our minds have wandered off somewhere else. Even though a passage may be familiar, however, we should realize that it contains more depth of meaning than we already understand. We can always approach the words of Scripture, even familiar words, expecting to understand them more deeply.

As we continue in our reading of the Bible, even very familiar parts will take on new meaning. The Bible helps explain itself: greater familiarity with the whole of Scripture provides a greater understanding of its individual books and passages. For example, the title "the Lamb of God" (Jn 1:29, 36), that John the Baptist uses to introduce Jesus, is undoubtedly familiar to us. But until we have read enough of the Old Testament to catch the double resonance of the Passover lamb of Exodus (Ex 12:3-10) and of Isaiah's "lamb led to the slaughter" (Is 53:7), we will fail to catch the deepest significance of John the Baptist's reference.

We should also seek to better understand how familiar passages apply to our lives. As our lives change, Scripture's meaning for us will change. When we read as children, we understood as children. As we grow, our understanding grows — not only in the sense that we are capable of greater intellectual feats, but in the sense that our greater life experience equips us to plumb the greater depths of God's word. As we enter more fully into the mystery of the Word made flesh, his words to us take on greater meaning.

> The Bible helps explain itself: greater familiarity with the whole of Scripture provides a greater understanding of its individual books and passages.

The words of Scripture can also seem lifeless not because they are familiar but because they are obscure. Portions of Ezekiel and the book of Revelation, for example, will likely strike us as very strange — or the obscurity may lie not in the book itself but in its meaning for us. For example, we may utterly fail to see the relevance to our own lives of the bloody wars of the Old Testament. Similarly, the words of a long genealogy will seldom leap from the page.

The best strategy in such cases is simply to peacefully pass over what is obscure or what seems to lack relevance to our Christian life today. Often when we reread these same passages a year later, they will take on meaning for us. But rather than focus now on what we don't appreciate or understand, we should focus on what does have a meaning for us. We cannot expect to become knowledgeable of the whole of Scripture all at once. As our reading continues, our understanding will grow, and the obscure will begin to take on meaning.

Do not be sad because Scripture is greater than you. The thirsty man is happy to drink, but he should not be distressed because he is unable to drain the source. The fountain should conquer your thirst, but your thirst should not conquer the fountain!... Give thanks for what you have received and do not grumble for what remains. That which you have taken and carried away is your portion, and what is left is also your inheritance, too. What you have not been able to receive because of your weakness, receive at other times thanks to your perseverance. Do not... abandon that which you are able to receive only little by little.

— COMMENTARY ON THE DIATESSARON 1.9,
ATTRIBUTED TO ST. EPHREM THE SYRIAN,
A DOCTOR OF THE CHURCH (306-373)

This is not to say that we should not make a serious attempt to understand what we read. Nor does it mean that we should be quick to discard portions of Scripture as unimportant. Rather, our attitude must be one of humility, recognizing that we have a long way to go in understanding the Bible and patiently pursuing our reading of it. If the aim of our reading is to listen to the word of God speak to us, then what is of primary importance for us are those portions of the Bible that his Holy Spirit does make clear to us. While we may want to understand the whole of the

Bible, we should pursue this goal with patience and persever-ance. We shouldn't lose sight of the basic reason we are reading Scripture: we aren't trying to become an expert about a book, but to listen to the word of God speaking to us.

Our reading can also become sidetracked by questions or disputes about the meaning of certain passages. Perhaps we have heard someone claim that none of the miracles reported in the Bible ever happened. Or we may have encountered someone of just the opposite view, who believes in the literal truth of *every* word in the Bible. We can probably sort out the more extreme views and reject them. But what are we to do about the many difficult passages in Scripture, and how do we sort out the different interpretations that have been given to them?

We shouldn't become distracted by questions that we cannot answer, or issues that we cannot solve. A healthy dose of humility is the safest course, admitting that we simply don't know the answers to all questions. We should persevere in our reading despite what we do not know. We can take comfort in the fact that many disputes over different interpretations of the Bible deal with issues that have little real bearing on our lives.

Still, there are questions whose answers are important, that bear on what we should believe and how we should live. Proper study of the Bible and about the Bible is indispensable for proper reading of the Bible. We cannot read Scripture as the word of God unless we take his word seriously enough to study it. That is the subject of the next chapter.

Resources

There are various monthly publications that provide daily Scripture reading guides. Two Catholic publications are:

- *God's Word Today* magazine, a daily Scripture reading guide that goes through the Bible book by book, with some months devoted to certain biblical themes. Over time, all the books of the Bible are read. Along with articles, each issue contains a "Daily Reading Guide" that assigns a Scripture reading for each day and provides a short commentary to help explain and apply the reading. For current subscription information and price, log on to www.godswordtoday.com, or call 1-800-246-7390.

- *The Word Among Us* magazine, which follows the lectionary readings with a one-page meditation for each day of the month. Articles explore various aspects of the Christian life and Catholic heritage. *The Word Among Us* is available in two English-language editions, one with the daily Mass readings. It is also published in a Spanish-language edition, *La Palabra entre Nosotros*. For current subscription information and prices log on to www.wau.org, or call 1-800-775-9673.

Study Guide

1. Why am I interested in reading the Bible? What is drawing me to Scripture?

2. Have I ever experienced God speaking his word to me? How?

3. How often do I read the Bible now? Every day? Most every day? Once a week? Occasionally? Rarely?

4. Can I commit myself to daily reading at a set time each day, at least for a trial period of one month?

5. Do I tend to read Scripture in big chunks? Or do I usually read a few verses at a time and meditate on them? Or do I do something in between? How well does my approach work for me?

6. What time each day for reading the Bible will work best for me?

7. What translation(s) of the Bible do I own? What translation(s) do I use most often? Am I satisfied with it (them)?

8. What words would I use to ask the Holy Spirit to help me as I read Scripture?

9. What is my track record at keeping my resolutions? Am I committed to making a sustained effort to read Scripture every day?

TWO

Understanding

Now there was an Ethiopian eunuch, a court official of the Candace, that is, the queen of the Ethiopians, in charge of her entire treasury, who had come to Jerusalem to worship, and was returning home. Seated in his chariot, he was reading the prophet Isaiah. The Spirit said to Philip, "Go and join up with that chariot." Philip ran up and heard him reading Isaiah the prophet and said, "Do you understand what you are reading?" He replied, "How can I, unless someone instructs me?" So he invited Philip to get in and sit with him.

— Acts 8:27-31

How often have we felt like this Ethiopian as we read Scripture? Our hearts are yearning, our minds alert — yet somehow the meaning of the words eludes us. We reread a passage and still its meaning isn't clear. We wish we had Philip by our side to interpret obscure passages and answer our questions.

The Ethiopian may not appear to be the kind of person who would need help in understanding Scripture. As an important court official, he was intelligent and well educated. He could read Hebrew or Greek as well as his native language. His worshipping in Jerusalem indicates that he was a God-fearing man who had come on pilgrimage to the Temple.

Furthermore, the Ethiopian was dedicated enough to read Scripture while traveling on a crude road in a chariot without any kind of spring suspension. His reading Scripture in a jolting chariot suggests that he was seriously interested in learning its meaning. Even so, he did not understand what he was reading, and needed Philip's assistance.

Luke presents this episode as if it can be taken for granted that the words of Scripture can be difficult to understand. He presents the Ethiopian as an eager reader, but one who needs help to make sense out of the book of Isaiah.

We should note how the Holy Spirit helped him. The Spirit did not directly enlighten the mind of the Ethiopian, but providentially arranged a hitchhiker who could explain the meaning of Isaiah. Philip was one human being helping another human being understand Scripture.

> The Spirit did not directly enlighten the mind of the Ethiopian, but providentially arranged a hitchhiker who could explain the meaning of Isaiah.

Sometimes, we may be aware of the promptings and help of the Holy Spirit as we read Scripture and pray. But the Spirit will generally make use of various natural guides and means to help us understand the words of Scripture — even, at times, sending help through another person who can share her or his insights.

> The books of both the Old and New Testaments in their entirety, with all their parts, are sacred and canonical because written under the inspiration of the Holy Spirit, they have God as their author.
>
> — *Divine Revelation*, no. 11

Understanding the Inspired Meaning of Scripture

Our aim in reading Scripture must be to understand the inspired sense of what we read. The Holy Spirit inspired the writing of the books of Scripture, making God in a real sense the author of Scripture. God revealed himself through word and deed to the Israelite people; in the fullness of time God revealed himself most fully through Jesus Christ. "In times past, God spoke in partial and various ways to our ancestors through the prophets; in these last days, he spoke to us through a son" (Heb 1:1-2). The books of Scripture are the written testimony to God's encounter with his people and his revelation through his Son.

> In composing the sacred books, God chose men and while employed by Him they made use of their powers and abilities, so that with Him acting in them and through them, they, as true authors, consigned to writing everything and only those things which He wanted. Therefore, since everything asserted by the inspired authors or sacred writers must be held to be asserted by the Holy Spirit, it follows that the books of Scripture must be acknowledged as teaching solidly, faithfully and without error that truth which God wanted put into sacred writings for the sake of salvation.
>
> — *DIVINE REVELATION*, NO. 11

While God is the author of Scripture, its pages did not drop down from heaven like manna. Nor did angels dictate the words of Scripture to human secretaries. Rather, the Holy Spirit inspired men (and women!) to speak the word of God as prophets, to recount God's dealings with his people, to edit what had been handed down from earlier sources, to write the words that we read in the Bible. Some of the biblical authors were aware that the Holy Spirit was prompting them to speak on behalf of God: "Then the spirit of the LORD fell upon me, and he told me to say: Thus says the LORD" (Ez 11:5). Other biblical authors give their readers no indication that they thought they were writing under the inspiration of the Holy Spirit. The author of 2 Maccabees says that he condensed a five-volume work by an earlier writer into a single volume in order "to please those who prefer simple reading" (2 Mac 2:23-32; see also 15:37-39). Luke describes his efforts as that of a careful researcher (Lk 1:1-4). Whether or not a biblical author was aware of the Holy Spirit's inspiration is of little importance; what is important is that the Spirit did guide these authors so that they wrote what God wanted written. As the Second Vatican Council proclaimed, the biblical authors were "true authors" (*Divine Revelation*, no. 11), making use of their skills as they wrote, perhaps searching (like any author) for the right words to express what needed expressing.

But while the human authors are "true authors" of the books of Scripture, so also do these books "have God as their author" (*Divine Revelation*, no. 11). How the books of the Bible have both God and humans as their authors without compromising either divine authorship or human authorship is a mystery. It is related to another great mystery, the mystery of Jesus Christ being both fully human and fully divine. Just as we must accept Jesus as fully divine and fully human, so we must accept the words of Scripture as words of God and words of humans. I will say more about this in Chapter 5.

> For the words of God, expressed in human language, have been made like human discourse, just as the word of the eternal Father, when He took to Himself the flesh of human weakness, was in every way made like men.
>
> — *DIVINE REVELATION*, NO. 13

This means that while we read Scripture to hear the word of God, to understand Scripture we must understand the words of humans. God speaks to us in Scripture through a chorus of voices, each of them distinctive. We must hear each voice and grasp what it is saying in order to understand what God is saying. We must hear the whole choir of voices in order to appreciate the harmony of God's word to us in Scripture. We must pay attention to the human to hear the divine.

The first step in understanding Scripture is to read carefully and attentively, trying to fathom the meaning of what we read. If we are reading a passage from Paul, we try to understand the point he is trying to make. Many passages of Scripture convey meaning to us even on a first reading. Some passages that at first glance may seem obscure take on meaning as we go through them slowly and analyze them.

> The first step in understanding Scripture is to read carefully and attentively, trying to fathom the meaning of what we read.

Sometimes, however, we will find ourselves in the sandals of the Ethiopian. Although he was intelligent and dedicated, he was trying to understand a text from a language and a culture that were not his own. It is hard for anyone to cross cultural and language lines and grasp nuances of meaning. The Bible comes from an age long past and cultures quite different from our own, and is written in languages with idioms that sound strange to us ("my horn is exalted in my God" — 1 Sam 2:1). Good translations can bridge the language gap for us, to a point. But we must also bridge the cultural gap between us and the people that God chose to reveal himself to and through. We must pick up, bit by bit, a knowledge of the biblical world and its customs and practices. Some we will absorb over time as we read the Bible. Some we need to have explained to us by footnotes or commentaries.

For example, we need to know something about marriage customs at the time of Jesus to understand the situation of Joseph and Mary:

> When his mother Mary was betrothed to Joseph, but before they lived together, she was found with child through the holy Spirit. Joseph her husband, since he was a righteous man, yet unwilling to expose her to shame, decided to divorce her quietly.
>
> — Mt 1:18-19

First-century Jewish marriage involved two stages: betrothal and living together. Once a woman was betrothed to a man, they were bound to each other as husband and wife even though the wife continued to live with her parents and the couple did not have sexual relations. Mary and Joseph were in the first stage of their marriage when she was found to be pregnant, and he decided to divorce her rather than have her move into his house. Many of Matthew's first readers were Jewish Christians who understood Jewish marriage customs. We need a little help to be able to understand Matthew's Gospel as his first readers understood it.

> Our goal is to understand what the words of Scripture conveyed when they were written, which means understanding the Scriptures as did those for whom they were first written.

Our goal is to understand what the words of Scripture conveyed when they were written, which means understanding the Scriptures as did those for whom they were first written. The inspired sense of the words of Scripture is the "meaning the sacred writers really intended, and what God wanted to manifest by means of their words" (*Divine Revelation*, no. 12). The human authors of Scripture wrote for the readers of their day. Paul's letters to Corinth were written to guide the church in Corinth in the middle of the first century. His letters can also guide us, for they were written under the inspiration of the Holy Spirit and contain God's word to us. But they were written to Corinthians and dealt with problems faced by the Corinthian church. Sometimes, their problems are not our problems, so we have to learn a bit of background to understand what is at issue. For example, Paul devotes three chapters to the question of whether Christians were free in conscience to eat meat from animals that had been offered as sacrifices to pagan gods (1 Cor 8-10). This isn't a problem for us today, but there is a message for us in how Paul resolves the question. We have to understand the meaning that his words conveyed to the Corinthians in a first-century setting to understand the meaning they have as God's word for us today.

> However, since God speaks in Sacred Scripture through men in human fashion, the interpreter of Sacred Scripture, in order to see clearly what God wanted to communicate to us, should carefully investigate what meaning the sacred writers really intended, and what God wanted to manifest by means of their words.
>
> — *DIVINE REVELATION,* NO. 12

We must study the Scriptures if we are to understand their meaning and be able to listen to the word of God speak to us through them. A lesson that we can learn from the Ethiopian is that God does not speak to us so simply through Scripture that we can expect to immediately and correctly understand every passage that we read. We must be willing to make an effort to understand the message of Scripture.

Our study of the Bible is part of our taking Scripture seriously. We must be willing to let our lives be shaped by what Scripture teaches; we also must be committed to discovering just what it teaches. If we are content to take the first meaning that pops into our head as the meaning of Scripture, we risk arriving at mistaken interpretations and we show a disregard for Scripture. If Scripture has been inspired by God for our reading and instruction, we must respect it enough to be willing to study it.

> We try to understand what we read in Scripture so that we can listen clearly to the word of God speaking to us through the words of Scripture.

We should always keep the goal of study in mind. We try to understand what we read in Scripture so that we can listen clearly to the word of God speaking to us through the words of Scripture. We don't study so that we can become experts in the Bible in the way that, for example, some people are experts in the history of the American Civil War. Our study is for the sake of our prayerful use of Scripture, so that we may encounter the Word of God there, and find life in that word.

Principles for Understanding Scripture

Our goal in reading any book is to understand what its author is conveying by his or her words. The goal of Scripture study is the same: to understand Scripture is to understand what its divine and human authors conveyed by the words they used. A passage of Scripture, first of all, means what the authors expressed when they wrote it. There can be extended meanings and interpretations given to passages, meanings which go beyond what the authors had in mind. But, however valid such interpretations may be, they are not the basic meaning of the passage. The basic meaning is that which is conveyed by the author. All additional or extended interpretations must be based upon this fundamental meaning and be extensions of it.

Paul intended to convey something to the Corinthians when he wrote his letters to them. Because Paul wrote under the inspiration of the Holy Spirit, what he intended to convey and what God intended to convey were the same.

For example, Paul intended to convey something to the Corinthians when he wrote his letters to them. Because Paul wrote under the inspiration of the Holy Spirit, what he intended to convey and what God intended to convey were the same. God did not use Paul to teach something that Paul himself did not understand, or something he was not aware that he was saying. Paul himself insisted that "for we write you nothing but what you can read and understand, and I hope that you will understand completely" (2 Cor 1:13). Thus, Paul should be able to understand and agree with the interpretation we give to his letters to Corinth.

An important step in grasping the meaning conveyed by the authors is to understand the sense in which they used words.

When the psalms call upon God as a "rock" (Ps 18:3, 32, 47; 62:7-8), they obviously don't intend that God be pictured as an actual rock. Rather, they want "rock" to be understood in a figurative sense, conveying an impression of the steadfast reliability of God. Therefore, in our reading of Scripture, we need to understand whether the authors intended their words to have a literal or a figurative meaning.

What is true of individual words and phrases is reflected in larger portions of Scripture as well. Not every story in the Bible is intended to be a historical account of an actual event. When Jesus said, "A man fell victim to robbers as he went down from Jerusalem to Jericho" (Lk 10:30), he was teaching by means of a parable — a fictional incident. To ask whether the incident really happened is to miss the point. The message Jesus wanted to teach has to do with love of neighbor; he was not giving the latest Jericho road crime report.

The book of Jonah may be read as an extended parable. There is no trace in other biblical documents, or in Assyrian documents of the time, of any conversion of Nineveh and its king to the God of Israel. Excavations have revealed that Nineveh was a city of no more than three square miles, not such "an enormously large city" that "it took three days to go through it" (Jon 3:3). Even leaving the matter of the great fish aside, it seems clear that the author of Jonah was not trying to write history.

The author of Jonah wanted to teach something about God's mercy and willingness to forgive. He wanted to correct the narrow nationalism of some Jews after their return from exile, and to show that God's love extended even to non-Jews. To ask whether Jonah was really swallowed by a fish is like asking whether a man was really robbed on the Jericho road.

> In our reading of Scripture, we need to understand whether the authors intended their words to have a literal or a figurative meaning.

> To ask whether Jonah was really swallowed by a fish is like asking whether a man was really robbed on the Jericho road.

Such questions miss the point the author intended to make, and hence misunderstand the message inspired by God.

We must therefore make an effort to detect the different types of writing used by the authors of Scripture — what are called "literary forms." Different books of the Bible were written in different ways for different purposes. The Bible contains books of history, books of prayer, books of advice, books of rules, books setting down the good news of what God did in Jesus Christ. Sometimes, the same book will contain different kinds of writings.

> To search out the intention of the sacred writers, attention should be given, among other things, to "literary forms." For truth is set forth and expressed differently in texts which are variously historical, prophetic, poetic, or of other forms of discourse. The interpreter must investigate what meaning the sacred writer intended to express and actually expressed in particular circumstances by using contemporary literary forms in accordance with the situation of his own time and culture. For the correct understanding of what the sacred author wanted to assert, due attention must be paid to the customary and characteristic styles of feeling, speaking and narrating which prevailed at the time of the sacred writer, and to the patterns men normally employed at that period in their everyday dealings with one another.
>
> — *Divine Revelation*, no. 12

The Bible is not a seamless garment. It is a quilt cut of many different kinds of cloth, woven in different stitches, and sewn together over a period of centuries. The design of the quilt is God's, but the weavers and the cutters and the sewers were human. We cannot hop from one part of the quilt to another and expect to find the same fabric in the same color in the same weave.

Although bound between two covers, the Bible is not a book but a library of books. Some of the books in this library were written as a kind of history. The books of 1 and 2 Kings fall into this category. But they aren't written as a modern historian would write history: the Hebrew historian was much more interested in the significance of events than in accurately recording the details of what happened. Some parts of the Bible, like the first eleven chapters of Genesis, may look like history but are really something quite different. The authors and editors of Genesis wished to teach about the condition of the human race and its relationship to God. They did not intend to teach, and were not inspired to teach, about the cosmic and geological processes of creation

Not even all of Paul's epistles are cut from the same cloth. His letter to Philemon is a genuine letter, written from one person to another, much as we would write a letter today. However, Paul's letter to Rome more resembles a doctrinal essay than a personal letter.

The forms of writing in the Bible are as varied as the forms of writing in a popular magazine. When we read a magazine, we know that it will contain articles that intend to present facts and information. It may also contain short stories — not meant to present factual information but to provide entertainment or insight. It may contain poetry, with dazzling visual imagery. It may contain an editorial, whose purpose will not be to present objective information in a detached manner but to convince us of a point of view. It will also contain ads, designed to get us to buy something.

If we confuse these different types of writing, the magazine will leave us in a muddle. But we don't: we know that the exaggerated claims of ads must be taken with a grain of salt. We apply very different criteria to factual articles, opinionated editorials, fictional short stories, and lyrical poetry.

Sometimes, we tend to read the Bible with less sophistication than that with which we read popular magazines. We lump together vastly different kinds of writing as if they were all the same, written by a single hand at a single sitting. But God in his generosity has given us an entire library, written over a period of almost 1,000 years, by many hands in many different literary forms. God's generosity makes demands on us, the readers of the library.

We must take care to understand what the inspired authors were trying to express and the way they expressed it.

Sometimes, we tend to read the Bible with less sophistication than that with which we read popular magazines. We lump together vastly different kinds of writing as if they were all the same, written by a single hand at a single sitting.

Unless we have some basic appreciation for the kind of biblical book we are reading and the inspired intent of the author in writing it, our understanding of Scripture will remain superficial and our ability to listen to God speak to us through its words will be hampered. We may confuse our misinterpretations for his voice.

Practical Steps to Understanding Scripture

We might begin study of a book of Scripture by reading a brief introduction to it, either in the edition of the Bible that we are using or in a book that discusses the books of Scripture. We might then read the book of Scripture itself as a whole.

Our basic approach, however, to reading a book of Scripture should be to go through it section by section during our fifteen minutes of daily Scripture reading. We might read a passage through from beginning to end, getting the general meaning. Then we can go back and reread it slowly, verse by verse, paying particular attention to the meaning. We might make use of study aids, such as footnotes in the edition of the Bible that we are using or commentaries.

Many people find it helpful to mark certain verses or passages as they read, underlining important words or highlighting certain sections by drawing a line alongside them in the margin. There is nothing irreverent in marking up our Bibles. The word of God is best honored by the place we give it in our minds and hearts, not the place we give it on a living room table. We'll want to mark cautiously, however; the passage we heavily underline with ballpoint pen today might not be the passage that speaks meaningfully to us tomorrow. It's better to use pencil and mark lightly, leaving room to mark something else the next time we read the same passage.

> There is nothing irreverent in marking up our Bibles. The word of God is best honored by the place we give it in our minds and hearts, not the place we give it on a living room table.

As we read, the questions that should be foremost in our minds are, "What point is the author trying to make? What is being conveyed?" These are questions that are unconsciously in our minds when we read most things, whether an editorial in a newspaper, instructions for assembling a tricycle, or a magazine article on heart disease. Our first approach to understanding the Bible should be the same: we read in order to grasp what is written. If we are overawed by the holiness of God's word, and strain too hard to hear what God is saying to us, we may miss the obvious meaning that the words themselves convey. Yet the words themselves must be the starting point in our understanding Scripture and listening to God speak to us through it. In one sense, we must first read the Bible as we would read any other book in order to experience the reality that the Bible is *unlike* any other book.

We should pay attention to the context in which individual verses and passages occur. Reading out of context can distort or destroy meaning. We should be alert to the broad context of the entire Bible. Each book finds its setting and meaning within the work of God that began with Abraham and continues in the Church. The Bible is a testimony to that work of God, and each book in it captures some segment or aspect of it. As we read a passage or book, we should be alert to the light that other passages and books throw upon what we are reading.

> But, since Holy Scripture must be read and interpreted in the sacred spirit in which it was written, no less serious attention must be given to the content and unity of the whole of Scripture if the meaning of the sacred texts is to be correctly worked out. The living tradition of the whole Church must be taken into account along with the harmony which exists between elements of the faith.
>
> — *DIVINE REVELATION*, NO. 12

As we read, we should put ourselves at the scene of what we are reading. If we are reading a passage from the Gospels, we should note not only what Jesus taught, but to whom he taught it and what their reaction was. We might imagine what our reaction would have been had we been on the scene ourselves — sometimes those who first listened to Jesus were astonished by sayings we read quite calmly today: "Then many of his disciples who were listening said, 'This saying is hard; who can accept it?'"(Jn 6:60). Perhaps we're missing something that should astonish us. Do we too easily pass over hard sayings of Jesus as if they didn't apply to us?

If we are reading one of the Old Testament prophets, we should keep in mind the condition of God's people at the time the prophet was speaking. The prophets spoke God's word to specific situations at different times in Israel's history. Were the people unfaithful to God, with destruction of the nation looming — or was the prophet speaking a word of comfort to a people in exile?

We also need to continually learn from the Bible about the life and culture of ancient times and let that knowledge enlighten our further reading. Biblical references to water and streams take on fuller meaning when we realize that the Israelites spent their earliest years wandering in the desert, living from water hole to water hole, and that water was still a precious commodity in the land God gave his people. The familiar verse about not lighting a lamp and putting it under a bushel basket, but upon a stand where it can give light to all in the house (Mt 5:15), becomes more vivid when we realize that many families lived in one-room houses.

Our study about the Bible shouldn't replace our basic daily fifteen-minute Scripture reading; both require time of their own.

We don't have to make a study of ancient life and culture as much as be attentive to the clues contained in Scripture itself to absorb a feeling for what life was like in biblical times. Our aim is not to become experts about the ancient world but to appreciate the meaning that Jesus' words had for their first listeners. In order to listen to the word of God speak to us in the twenty-first century, we must strive to listen to the prophets as did sixth-century B.C. inhabitants of Jerusalem, sit at the feet of Jesus as first-century disciples, and put ourselves in the congregations to whom Paul wrote.

In addition to our fifteen minutes of daily Scripture reading, we may want to periodically spend some time in study *about* the Bible. Occasionally reading books that deal with biblical topics and themes is very helpful if our understanding of Scripture is to mature and grow. Of course, our study about the Bible shouldn't replace our basic daily fifteen-minute Scripture reading; both require time of their own.

Aids for Understanding

There are many resources available for our study of Scripture.

The first resource for our study is the Bible itself. The Bible explains itself, in the sense that a familiarity with the whole of Scripture will make the individual books and passages easier to understand. As we grow in our understanding of the Old Testament, our understanding of the New Testament will take on greater depth. As we learn more about the customs and culture of first-century Palestine, the words and actions of Jesus will take on more meaning for us. As we become acquainted with all of Paul's missionary activities described in the Acts of the Apostles, his individual letters will become easier to understand.

Many editions of the Bible include cross-references to other portions of the Bible that relate to the passage being read. Looking up these cross-references is a simple means of Scripture study. Cross-references are plentiful for the Gospels of Matthew, Mark, and Luke, since many incidents and teachings from the life of Jesus are included in two or three of these Gospels. Different Gospel writers present the same incident with different emphases; comparing two or three accounts highlights the messages that each author wishes to convey.

> The first resource for our study is the Bible itself. The Bible explains itself, in the sense that a familiarity with the whole of Scripture will make the individual books and passages easier to understand.

Sometimes, cross-references in the New Testament point to the location of a passage in the Old Testament that is being quoted or invoked by Jesus or a New Testament writer. Looking up the Old Testament passage and reading it in its original context can often help us better understand the point that Jesus or Paul is making.

Another convenient resource for our study are the footnotes provided in various editions of the Bible. Among the more useful footnotes are those that clarify obscure passages. It can often be helpful to glance at the footnotes for a chapter before beginning to read the chapter; one or two of the notes may stand out as worth particular attention. If we already have a general familiarity with the particular Scripture reading we are doing that day, we might want to study these notes right away, so that our later reading of the words of Scripture can be uninterrupted.

Many editions of the Bible contain maps that provide the lay of the land in which biblical events occurred. A map of

Palestine at the time of Jesus reveals, for example, that the villages of Capernaum, Chorazin, and Bethsaida, "where most of his mighty deeds had been done" (Mt 11:20), lay within two to four miles of each other. Jesus apparently paid a lot of attention to three villages an hour's walk from each other. Paul, on the other hand, traveled thousands of miles, as shown in maps of his missionary journeys.

Another convenient resource for our study are the footnotes provided in various editions of the Bible.

We can inadvertently undermine the power of Scripture by treating it as a collection of writings from another world, one with no connection to our own. To bridge that gap, we can match up the cities and countries of the Bible with modern cities and countries. Jerusalem is Jerusalem and Rome is Rome, of course. But do we consciously realize when we read of Paul's first journey that he was traveling mostly through the modern country of Turkey? Do we locate Old Testament events that took place in Babylon and Persia as occurring in the modern countries of Iraq and Iran? Making such connections can remind us that the word of God was spoken in our world, that Jesus Christ walked among us, that what we read in Scripture is a word addressed to our world... and to us.

We can inadvertently undermine the power of Scripture by treating it as a collection of writings from another world, one with no connection to our own. To bridge that gap, we can match up the cities and countries of the Bible with modern cities and countries.

To grow in our understanding of the individual books of Scripture, we'll want to consult study aids as well. It's helpful, for example, to use a resource that discusses what type of literature a given book of Scripture is, the background of its composition (to the extent that this is known), and its main concerns and themes. Making use of such a study aid before reading (or rereading) a book of the Bible can lay the groundwork for greater understanding by preparing us for what we will find there.

Perhaps it's unnecessary to repeat that such study aids about the Bible should never replace reading of Scripture itself — but neither should such study aids be shunned. If we were to take a summer trip with our family to visit the historic sites of the American Civil War, we'd probably consult a map beforehand and carry a guidebook with brief explanations of the major battle sites. Reading a map or guidebook can never replace making the actual trip, but it can help us find our way to where we want to go. What may only appear to be a grassy meadow can, with the help of additional information, come alive to us when we visit it as a historical battlefield.

> Having some idea of the nature of a book of Scripture can help us avoid getting lost in it, and knowing something about the authors' concerns can help us better understand the significance of what they wrote.

So, too, with Scripture. Although "tour guides" and background information are no substitute for Scripture reading itself, having some idea of the nature of a book of Scripture can help us avoid getting lost in it, and knowing something about the authors' concerns can help us better understand the significance of what they wrote.

The most convenient study aids are the introductions to the individual books of Scripture provided in many editions of the Bible. These vary in quality and scope, but can give the reader some orientation to what he or she is about to read, and shouldn't be overlooked. A good introduction can go a long way in making a book of the Old Testament intelligible, if only by providing the setting in which the book was written. To return to the analogy of the Bible as a quilt: it is often enlightening to know when a particular square of cloth was woven, and by whom, and in what setting. The literary form of the book of Daniel has important differences from the literary form of the books of Kings. Adequate introductions can alert us to the unique character of each book, and help us avoid falling into a "Bible-as-seamless-garment" mentality.

Commentaries and books about Scripture should also have a place in our study. It is naïve to assume that twenty-first-century Americans can intuitively grasp the distinctive culture of the Israelite people of 2,500 years ago, or the political and religious culture of the first-century Judaism in which Jesus exercised his ministry. If the Bible contains the revelation of God in words of human beings, we must strive to understand those words as words of actual people. Like the Ethiopian, we must make a pilgrimage to Jerusalem. The word of God came to the human race through specific individuals within a specific people — and finally through the specific person of Jesus Christ.

Now for all time, all nations and all people must turn to these writings as the privileged source of God's revelation. Whatever the obstacles of language or culture, whatever the distance created by time and geography, we must enter into the world of Moses and Isaiah, Jesus and Paul, to learn of God's intervention into human history. Reference works about Scripture can provide an indispensable help for us in doing this.

> Whatever the distance created by time and geography, we must enter into the world of Moses and Isaiah, Jesus and Paul, to learn of God's intervention into human history.

A dictionary of the Bible, providing information about specific topics and words, can be a handy and inexpensive reference work for us to consult.

Concordances list the different places a given word is used in the Bible and can help us locate passages (where does Isaiah talk about a lamb?) or study some biblical themes. Each translation of the Bible must have its own concordance, since different translations translate words differently.

Many commentaries on the books of the Bible are available, providing an introduction to each book and a verse-by-verse (or even phrase-by-phrase) explanation of that book.

Other books deal with biblical topics (for example, fasting in the Bible) or concerns (for example, the call to establish justice and peace).

Browsing through a bookstore that carries Catholic Bibles and books can be a way of finding materials suited to your needs and interests. More and more resources are becoming available online for purchase as well.

Study needn't distract us from hearing God's word, but it can be a step toward hearing God's word more clearly. In the end, though, study must give way to listening — the subject of the next chapter.

Resources

The *Catechism of the Catholic Church* addresses the human and divine authorship of Scripture and its inspiration in sections 101-114.

There are many resources to help us understand Scripture; the following are only a smattering. Some of these and other resources are available from amazon.com or christianbook.com.

- The *New American Bible,* the *New Jerusalem Bible,* and the *New Revised Standard Version* are available in editions that contain introductions to the books of the Bible and footnotes.

- *The Catholic Study Bible* (Oxford University Press) contains the text of the New American Bible along with 100 pages of articles on biblical topics and 400 pages of extended introductions for the individual books of the Bible.

- The *Dictionary of the Bible* by John McKenzie (Touchstone Books), published in 1965, is a classic. It contains a wealth of information and is available in paperback.

- *The Collegeville Bible Commentary* (The Liturgical Press) is a basic one-volume commentary on all the books of the Bible. The *New Collegeville Bible Commentary: New Testament* contains new commentaries on the books of the New Testament.

- Considerably more detailed is the one-volume *New Jerome Bible Commentary* (Prentice Hall) In addition to a commentary on the entire Bible, it has discussions of each book of the Bible and more than twenty scholarly essays.
- There are many commentaries on individual books of the Bible, frequently published in series. One new series is the *Catholic Commentary on Sacred Scripture* (Baker Academic) written by various authors. It covers the books of the New Testament and has a theological and pastoral focus.
- My own *Bringing the Gospel of Matthew to Life* and *Bringing the Gospel of Mark to Life* (available on amazon.com) provide a verse-by-verse explanation of these Gospels and aim at leading the reader to reflection and prayer. They each contain some eighty-five blocks of information about first-century life, religious beliefs, and institutions, as well as other background for understanding the Gospels.
- *The Bible Today* magazine (The Liturgical Press) is published bimonthly and contains non-technical articles on Scripture. It began publication in 1962 and is the premier American Catholic biblical magazine. Information available at www.litpress.org or 1-800-858-5450.
- Printed concordances are giving way to searchable versions of the Bible on CDs or Web sites. The *Deluxe Bible 3.1* is a CD-ROM containing the text of the *New American Bible* and has the capability to do word searches; as I write, it is available from www.catholiccompany.com. The oremus Bible Browser Web site allows one to do word searches through the *New Revised Standard Version* — http://bible.oremus.org.
- There are free biblical resources and study aids on many Web sites, with new sites appearing constantly and old ones lapsing. Some of the Catholic-sponsored sites are:

http://catholic-resources.org/
http://www.salvationhistory.com/
http://catholicbiblestudent.com/

- A Web site with links to Catholic Church documents related to biblical studies: http://catholic-resources.org/ ChurchDocs.
- An academic Web site: http://ntgateway.com.

Each Web site contains links to other related sites. As with all Web browsing, viewer caution is advised. There is much good material on the Web… and some that's not so good!

Study Guide

1. Is the biblical world a foreign land for me, or do I feel at home in it?

2. Do I dread having to study, or do I enjoy learning new things? What was my last experience of acquiring a new skill — learning how to do something I did not know how to do before?

3. Does the prospect of studying the Bible appeal to me, or is it simply one more duty competing for my time? Am I personally convinced that reading the Bible as God's word demands some study?

4. When I read the Bible, do I try to grasp the meaning that the inspired authors of Scripture intended their words to have? How might I more sharply focus on that meaning?

5. Some of the types of writing (or literary forms) used in the Bible are prayers, parables, letters, and history. What other types of writing have I found in the Bible?

6. What book of the Bible am I now reading or am I about to read? What simple steps might I take to enrich my reading by a little study of this biblical book?

7. Can I think of an example of how examining the context of a particular Scripture passage helped me better understand it?

8. What study aids are included in the edition of the Bible that I read? Which of these study aids do I make use of when I read Scripture?

9. What other Scripture study aids do I have at my disposal? Which of them have I found helpful? What kind of help did they give me? What other study aid might help me better understand Scripture?

THREE

Listening

Now that very day two of them were going to a village seven miles from Jerusalem called Emmaus, and they were conversing about all the things that had occurred. And it happened that while they were conversing and debating, Jesus himself drew near and walked with them, but their eyes were prevented from recognizing him. . . .

And he said to them, "Oh, how foolish you are! How slow of heart to believe all that the prophets spoke! Was it not necessary that the Messiah should suffer these things and enter into his glory?" Then beginning with Moses and all the prophets, he interpreted to them what referred to him in all the scriptures. . . .

And it happened that, while he was with them at table, he took bread, said the blessing, broke it, and gave it to them. With that their eyes were opened and they recognized him, but he vanished from their sight. Then they said to each other, "Were not our hearts burning [within us] while he spoke to us on the way and opened the scriptures to us?"

— Lk 24:13-16, 25-27, 30-32

We can assume that the disciples of Jesus were well acquainted with the Scriptures, the books that we read as the Old Testament. As devout Jews they had studied these books and made an effort to understand God's word. Yet despite this, and despite their close association with Jesus, they failed to understand that he fulfilled the Scriptures.

Jesus used their knowledge of the Scriptures as the basis for explaining his own mission. He interpreted the Scriptures, throwing new light on familiar passages, showing the connection between what the prophets foretold and his own life. Through Jesus' explanation, the two disciples not only came to a new understanding of Scripture; they came to a deeper understanding of Jesus himself. His words not only gave them enlightenment and knowledge; his words also touched their hearts. "Were not our hearts burning [within us] while he spoke to us on the way and opened the scriptures to us?" (Lk 24:32).

Jesus is by our side (see Mt 28:20). He will touch our hearts as we listen to him in our reading. We need to go about reading Scripture in such a way that he can speak to our hearts as well as our heads. We need to learn how to listen, and we need the inspiration of the Holy Spirit in our listening.

In Luke's Gospel, Jesus' first words during his public ministry are based on a passage from the prophet Isaiah (Lk 4:16-21; Is 61:1-2). Jesus made the bold claim, "Today this Scripture passage is fulfilled in your hearing" (Lk 4:21). His last words before he ascends into heaven also refer to the Scriptures: "He said to them, 'These are my words that I spoke to you while I was still with you, that everything written about me in the law of Moses and in the prophets and psalms must be fulfilled.' Then he opened their minds to understand the scriptures" (Lk 24:44-45).

Our hearts, too, would burn within us if Jesus would be at our side, opening our minds to the meaning of Scripture. We wish we could read the words of the Old Testament in such a way that Jesus would shine through them, so that we could share the understanding that the two disciples received as they walked the road to Emmaus with Jesus.

But Jesus *is* by our side (see Mt 28:20). He will touch our hearts as we listen to him in our reading. We need to go about reading Scripture in such a way that he can speak to our hearts as well as our heads. We need to learn how to listen, and we need the inspiration of the Holy Spirit in our listening.

Attitudes

To hear Jesus' voice as the disciples did, we must approach Scripture with the right attitudes of mind and heart. We must make an effort to understand the inspired meaning of the text, and we must approach Scripture with an eagerness to embrace the word we hear.

Listening to God speak to us through the words of Scripture requires putting our study in perspective. We need to study the books of the Bible much as we would study any other books, in order to gain an understanding of them. But study is not an end in itself. Rather, our study enables us to read Scripture with understanding so that we can listen to God speak to us through its words. We need to go beyond studying the Bible and simply read it as the word of God.

> Our study enables us to read Scripture with understanding so that we can listen to God speak to us through its words. We need to go beyond studying the Bible and simply read it as the word of God.

When we drive a car, we look through the windshield to see where we are going; we don't look at the windshield and make it the focus of our attention. A dirty windshield can obscure our vision, and we need to clean it. To do a good job at that, we will have to look at the windshield for a moment instead of looking through it.

Our study of the Bible is like cleaning the windshield. We need to look at the Bible in order to study it and grow in our understanding of it. We need to learn about each book of the Bible; we may need to compare translations to see how each one interprets difficult verses. But none of this is really reading Scripture as the word of God, anymore than looking at the windshield of a car is the same as looking through it. Study can even distract us from hearing God's word, just as staring at the bug spots on a windshield may cause us to drive off the road. We must get beyond our study of the Bible if we are to hear God speaking to us through the words of Scripture. The Bible must become for us a window to God.

The epistle of James uses a similar analogy in teaching us how to listen correctly to the word of God:

> Humbly welcome the word that has been planted in you and is able to save your souls. Be doers of the word and not hearers only, deluding yourselves. For if anyone is a hearer of the word and not a doer, he is like a man who looks at his own face in a mirror. He sees himself, then goes off and promptly forgets what he looked like.
>
> — JAS 1:21-24

We must get beyond our study of the Bible if we are to hear God speaking to us through the words of Scripture. The Bible must become for us a window to God.

Scripture can be a mirror in which we see and understand ourselves. It can give us a glimpse of ourselves in the eyes of God. But we must look at ourselves in the mirror, rather than at the mirror itself.

The fundamental attitude that we must bring to Scripture is an open heart: an eagerness to listen to the word of God and a willingness to heed it. If we want God to speak to us but aren't interested in really listening to him, we do him a discourtesy, just as we would be discourteous if we were to ask someone a question and then walk away in the middle of his or her answer. To want God to speak to us, but reserve our judgment on whether to take his words seriously, is to treat his voice as one opinion among many, not as the voice of God.

The fundamental attitude that we must bring to Scripture is an open heart: an eagerness to listen to the word of God and a willingness to heed it.

We should approach Scripture recognizing that God wishes to speak to each of us personally. The Bible is not a book that merely reveals something about God and his presence in history. If we read it properly, it is also a personal communication to each of us. The Holy Spirit is present in us, inspiring us when we read Scripture, so that God can speak to each of us as individuals.

> Therefore, as the holy Spirit says: "Oh, that today you would hear his voice."
>
> — HEB 3:7

When we check our mailbox each day, we find different kinds of mail in it. We receive ads addressed to Occupant. We receive bills that have our name on them, but that were sent to us by a computer. They are a more personal kind of mail than the Occupant letters, but we know that the computer is less interested in our names than in our account balances. We might receive a Christmas letter that a friend is sending to everyone on her Christmas card list. This letter is more personal than a bill, even though it was sent to a number of people besides ourselves. And finally, we might receive a letter from our father, or from a son or daughter. This letter, we would open first and read eagerly. It would be written and addressed to us in a truly personal way. It would be a greeting from someone who knows us very well and loves us.

> If we read Scripture as the word of God, we must read it as a letter that comes from our Father to us as individuals.

If we read Scripture as the word of God, we must read it as a letter that comes from our Father to us as individuals. The Bible is not addressed to "Occupant" as an ad for heaven sent to the human race. It is not impersonally addressed to us, like the bills and overdue notices sent by a computer. And, even though the Scriptures are for all men and women, God's voice does not address us all alike, as a Christmas newsletter does. God's voice speaks to each of us individually, as a father writes to each of his children by name.

Comparing Scripture to a personal letter gives us a clue to its deepest meaning. When a close friend or relative writes to us, they often tell us what is going on in their lives — perhaps the birth of a new child, perhaps moving to a new home, perhaps just simple events of daily life. Our friends and relatives don't wish to convey mere information about themselves as if we needed more facts to fill out a biography. The reason our friends write is to reveal themselves to us, because they love us and we love them. They send a letter not just to transmit a set of facts but to express themselves personally. Both the sending and the receiving of the letter have meaning because of the bond of love that exists between us and them. The letter is an expression of that love, and a means of allowing that love to grow.

So, too, with Scripture. God does not want to reveal facts so much as to reveal himself. He does not write to us because we are compiling his biography, but because he loves us and invites us to love him. Scripture is an expression of God himself and an expression of love for us. It is one of his means of personally inviting us to enter into a relationship of love with him. If we miss this basic focus, we miss the meaning of Scripture, no matter how well we might otherwise understand the Bible.

It is easy for us today to be merely spectators on life. We can watch images of floods and wars on the evening news, and get up to get a snack during the commercial. We are able to view terrifying events from a distance without having to get personally involved. This mere-observer attitude can unconsciously carry over into our reading of Scripture: we can read its words as true and important, but as not affecting us.

Personal involvement is different from detached observation. If we were driving along a deserted highway and were the first to arrive at the scene of a serious car accident, we would be thrust into the situation. We would be confronted with decisions: do we move the injured from their cars because of danger of fire, or would that aggravate their injuries? How do we stop serious bleeding? What should we do when someone is literally dying before our eyes? Our hearts would pound, our minds work feverishly to think of the right thing to do. How different it is to be there than to see a report of the accident on television!

Our encounter with the word of God in Scripture should be real and immediate to us. Not that our hearts should pound every time we read the Bible, but there should be a sense of immediacy about what we read. The Bible is not simply a report of what God said long ago, but contains the word of God being spoken to us here and now as we read. We cannot be detached observers; we must hear it as personally addressed to us, inviting our personal response.

> If we come before God eager to listen to what he would say to us — we will find that he does speak to us. We will read Scripture not as a dead letter, written long ago, but as a word spoken to us today.

If we bring to Scripture an attitude that it is God's word to us — if we come before God eager to listen to what he would say to us — we will find that he does speak to us. We will read Scripture not as a dead letter, written long ago, but as a word spoken to us today.

Approaches

We should approach Scripture in prayer. I mentioned earlier how important it is to begin our daily reading time with the prayer that God will speak to us through the words of Scripture; I can only emphasize this once again. We need to pray that God will speak to us through our reading of his word. Our prayer places us consciously in the presence of God. To listen to him speak through the words of Scripture, we need to be alone with him and his word, as free from distractions as possible, concentrating only on what he would say to us. If we are going to listen to his voice, we need to still all other voices, especially our mental wanderings. We don't need to strain to be alone with God's word; we should simply focus as best we can on him who is speaking to us.

"Be still and confess that I am God!"

— Ps 46:11

As we read Scripture, we should take the approach that "What I am reading is written to me. What I am reading is written about me." If we are reading the words of Jesus, we should read them as personally addressed to us. If we read a letter from Paul, we should read it as a letter written to us, as if it had been delivered in that day's mail.

As we read Scripture, we should take the approach that "What I am reading is written to me."

To apply Scripture so personally may seem unwarranted. But Paul uses Scripture this way in his letters, citing incidents in the Old Testament and applying them to the lives of those to whom he writes.

Paul wrote to the Corinthians:

> I do not want you to be unaware, brothers, that our ancestors were all under the cloud and all passed through the sea . . . Yet God was not pleased with most of them, for they were struck down in the desert. These things happened as examples for us, so that we might not desire evil things, as they did. . . . These things happened to them as an example, and they have been written down as a warning to us.
>
> — 1 Cor 10:1, 5-6, 11

Paul interprets Old Testament events as examples and warnings for his readers. Similarly, the events of both the Old and New Testaments are examples for us, instructing, warning, and encouraging.

Paul applies Old Testament texts to the lives of his readers. He writes the Corinthians, "It is written in the law of Moses,

'You shall not muzzle an ox while it is treading out the grain.' Is God concerned about oxen, or is he not really speaking for our sake? It was written for our sake, because the plowman should plow in hope, and the thresher in hope of receiving a share. If we have sown spiritual seed for you, is it a great thing that we reap a material harvest from you?" (1 Cor 9:9-11). Again, in his letter to Rome, Paul discusses Abraham's faith and maintains, "But it was not for him alone that it was written that 'it was credited to him'; it was also for us, to whom it will be credited, who believe in the one who raised Jesus our Lord from the dead" (Rom 4:23-24).

> If we read Scripture as Paul reads it, we will understand both what the text meant when the author wrote it and what it means for us personally.

If we read Scripture as Paul reads it, we will understand both what the text meant when the author wrote it and what it means for us personally. When we hear the word of God addressed to Israel through the prophet Jeremiah, saying, "With age-old love I have loved you" (Jer 31:3), we will understand these words to be God's assurance of his love for ancient Israel — their meaning when Jeremiah uttered them. But those words will also have a meaning for us today: we can listen to God speaking to us through those words, assuring us of his steadfast and everlasting love for us.

In the letter to the Ephesians, Paul prays for his readers, asking "that Christ may dwell in your hearts through faith; that you, rooted and grounded in love, may have strength to comprehend with all the holy ones what is the breadth and length and height and depth, and to know the love of Christ that surpasses knowledge, so that you may be filled with all the fullness of God" (Eph 3:17-19). The "you" Paul had in mind were Christians living in Ephesus two thousand years ago. But we can read Paul's words as words addressed to us, speaking about what God has in store for each one of us today. "What I am reading is written to me."

When we hear Jesus say, "Remove the wooden beam from your eye first; then you will see clearly to remove the splinter in your brother's eye" (Lk 6:42), some of our neighbors and their splinters may come to mind, and some of our own beams as well. When we hear Jesus say, "Stop judging and you will not be judged" (Lk 6:37), some of our own unfounded condemnations of others may occur to us, as well as the areas of our lives where we hope for mercy and not strict judgment. Above all, when we hear him say, "I came so that they might have life and have it more abundantly" (Jn 10:10), we will know that he is talking to us, saying that he came so that we may experience fullness of life. It is one thing for me to believe that Jesus came out of love for all women and men; it is another thing to accept that he loves me.

Our approach should be to read some sections of Scripture as being not so much spoken to *us* as *about* us.

Many of Jesus' sayings must be read as words addressed personally to us if we are to truly understand them. Jesus did not intend his teachings to be a body of abstract truths when he said things like "I am the resurrection and the life" (Jn 11:25). He intends that we hear his words as addressed specifically to us: "I am the resurrection and the life *for you*." Each of us is the *you* whom Jesus addresses.

Some of what we read in the Bible can be applied rather directly to our lives in this way; other parts, however, may be more difficult to apply. What are we to make of the passages and incidents that seem to have little to say to us in a personal way?

Our approach should be to read some sections of Scripture as being not so much spoken *to* us as *about* us. For example, the second book of Samuel tells how King David saw Bathsheba, the wife of Uriah the soldier, and desired her. David arranged for Uriah to be stationed at the front of the battle lines, where he was killed. The king then took Bathsheba as his own wife. This displeased God, who sent Nathan the prophet to David. Nathan told him a parable about a wealthy man who stole a poor man's single lamb. When David expressed his anger over the man's behavior, Nathan told David, "You are the man" (2 Sam 12:7).

The LORD sent Nathan to David, and when he came to him, he said: "Judge this case for me! In a certain town there were two men, one rich, the other poor. The rich man had flocks and herds in great numbers. But the poor man had nothing at all except one little ewe lamb that he had bought. He nourished her, and she grew up with him and his children. She shared the little food he had and drank from his cup and slept in his bosom. She was like a daughter to him. Now the rich man received a visitor but he would not take from his own flocks and herds to prepare a meal for the wayfarer who had come to him. Instead he took the poor man's ewe lamb and made a meal of it for his visitor." David's anger flared up and he said: "As the LORD lives, the man who has done this merits death. He shall restore the ewe lamb fourfold because he has done this and has had no pity." Then Nathan said to David, "You are the man."

— 2 SAM 12:1-7

We should say to ourselves as we read Scripture, "I am the man," or "I am the woman." What I read is written about *me*. It was not merely Peter who misunderstood Jesus and acted without thinking; I often misunderstand and act rashly. It was not only the priest and Levite in the parable of the good Samaritan who pass by the injured man on Jericho road (Lk 10:31-32); I do the same, every day. It was not only Lazarus whom Jesus loved and raised to life (Jn 11:36, 43-44); he loves me, and wishes to raise me to life.

Reading Scripture as speaking to us and about us makes it all the more important that we understand Scripture properly. If we misunderstand the point of a parable or teaching of Jesus, then we cannot properly apply it to our lives.

Yet it is also essential that the meaning of Scripture become a meaning *for us*. We can have keen insight into the parable of the good Samaritan, but we will not be reading it as the word of God for us unless we apply it to ourselves. Jesus asked the man to whom he first told the parable, "Which of these three, in your opinion, was neighbor to the robbers' victim?" (Lk 10:36). The answer was obvious: "The one who treated him with mercy" (Lk 10:37). Jesus then told him, "Go and do likewise" (Lk 10:37). We must hear Jesus' words to him as his word to us: go and do likewise, showing mercy on those who are in need of our mercy.

> We can have keen insight into the parable of the good Samaritan, but we will not be reading it as the word of God for us unless we apply it to ourselves.

Even seemingly obscure sections of the Old Testament can have their message for us. "For whatever was written previously was written for our instruction, that by endurance and by the encouragement of the scriptures we might have hope" (Rom 15:4). We should make an effort to understand every part of Scripture that we read as teaching us something about ourselves in the sight of God, and as conveying a message from God to us. We should be open to God speaking to us, even through unlikely passages.

God Speaks to Us

God will speak to those who prayerfully read the Bible as his word. He will not speak in an audible voice; he will speak to us through the words that we read. We will have a sense that the words of Scripture are indeed addressed to us and are talking about us; we will have a sense that they have a meaning and application in our own lives. The Bible will be not merely God's word, but God's word *to me*. Our hearts will burn within us as we read, not with violent emotion but with the gentle touch of the Holy Spirit, assuring us that the Father loves us and addresses us by name.

We cannot command God's speaking to us or stir up ourselves to make sure that something happens. Our part can only be to pray, to read with an open and attentive heart, to listen. It is God's part to do the speaking, to give understanding to our minds and touch our hearts. We cannot control his graces. It is a mistake to try to force an experience of God speaking to us, or to demand that he speak more dramatically than he chooses to.

There are times and seasons in all aspects of our spiritual lives. Some days the words of Scripture will seem to leap off the page. Other days they will lie there, dead, uninspiring. For perhaps weeks at a time we will read with understanding and insight; at other stretches our reading may be so unrewarding that only our resolve to continue faithfully will keep us going. Sometimes, the voice of the Lord will be one of comfort, consolation, care. At other times it will be a more severe voice, pointing out the price of discipleship, pointing out areas in our lives that must change. The voice of the Lord is both gentle and severe, as we need to hear it.

> God will speak to those who prayerfully read the Bible as his word. He will not speak in an audible voice; he will speak to us through the words that we read.

The Lord will not limit his speaking to us through the words of Scripture to the times that we are actually reading Scripture. In my own life, I find that I often hear God addressing me personally when I listen to the Scriptures being read during the celebration of the liturgy. Perhaps this is as it should be; perhaps our hearing of the word of God should be literally a *hearing*, and a hearing in the context of the Church gathered to listen to the word of God being proclaimed. I do know that the reading and study of Scripture that I do outside the liturgy has prepared me to listen to the word of God during the liturgy. It was only after I had been faithful to a daily time of reading and reflection on Scripture that the word of God proclaimed to me during the liturgy came alive.

I also find that the words of Scripture come alive for me at various times during the day when a thought from Scripture simply comes into my mind. The Lord speaks to me through his word by bringing passages to mind that are appropriate to the situation that I am in, or passages that contain a truth that I need to hear. My daily reading is still indispensable, for it provides the material that the Lord brings to my mind, and it enables me to understand the basic meaning and context of different passages from Scripture.

> In our reading, we enter into the world of Scripture so that the word of God may break into our world and our lives.

The important point is that we need to listen to the word of God addressed to us. Our faithful reading of Scripture plays an essential role in this, even on days when the words seem to lie lifeless on the page. The Lord will use our faithful reading to prepare us to listen to his word during the liturgy and to provide our minds with passages that he will later have us recall in particular situations. In our reading, we enter into the world of Scripture so that the word of God may break into our world and our lives.

Not every book in the Bible will speak to us equally clearly, or be equally enlightening to us. We shouldn't be afraid to admit to ourselves that there is much in the Bible that we do not understand, and that does not seem to speak to our situation. It is no disgrace if we find Leviticus less nourishing than the Gospel of John. One does not find every book in a library equally helpful or interesting at every moment — or even ever.

> While God wishes to speak with us on a daily basis, we should expect his voice to be most distinct at the turning points and critical junctures of our lives.

While God wishes to speak with us on a daily basis, we should expect his voice to be most distinct at the turning points and critical junctures of our lives. When we are most in need of guidance and assurance, we should have the greatest expectation of hearing the Lord's voice as we prayerfully turn to him.

Scripture played a critical role in the conversion of St. Augustine. One day when he was wrestling with his inability to forsake sins of the flesh, he heard a child's voice singing out, "Take it and read it, take it and read it." Augustine remembered that St. Anthony of the Desert had heard God speak to him through a passage in Scripture, changing his life. When Augustine opened up a Bible, his eyes fell on words that spoke to his heart in a way that swept aside doubt and indicated the path that he was to follow. It was the critical turning point in Augustine's life.

> Suddenly a voice reaches my ears from a nearby house . . . and the words are constantly repeated: "Take it and read it. Take it and read it." . . . I checked the force of my tears and rose to my feet, being quite certain that I must interpret this as a divine command to me to open the book and read the first passage which I should come upon. For I had heard this about Anthony: he had happened to come in when the Gospel was being read, and as though the words read were spoken directly to himself, had received the admonition: *Go, sell all that you have, and give to the poor, and you shall have treasure in heaven, and come and follow me* [Luke 18:22]. And by such an oracle he had been immediately converted . . . I snatched up the book, opened it, and read in silence the passage upon which my eyes first fell: *Not in reveling and drunkenness, not in debauchery and licentiousness, not in quarreling and jealousy. But put on the Lord Jesus Christ, and make no provision for the flesh, to gratify its desires* [Romans 13:13-14]. I had no wish to read further; there was no need to. For immediately I had reached the end of this sentence it was as though my heart was filled with a light of confidence and all the shadows of my doubt were swept away.
>
> — *CONFESSIONS* OF ST. AUGUSTINE, BOOK VIII, CHAPTER 12

God may speak more decisively at critical points in our lives, but we should expect that he will be present and will speak to us as a normal part of our daily reading of Scripture. Some days his voice may be more gentle than other days; some days his voice may seem to be stilled. But his voice will never be truly silent, if we but know how to listen for it.

The Holy Spirit

The inspiration of the Holy Spirit is essential to our reading Scripture as the word of God. Along with our efforts to understand Scripture and to read with an open heart, the Holy Spirit must be present as we read if we are to truly listen to God speak to us through the words of Scripture.

> The inspiration of the Holy Spirit is essential to our reading Scripture as the word of God.

We are given the Holy Spirit through our baptism into Jesus Christ. The Father adopts us as his sons and daughters and allows us to partake of his very life. As children of God, we are equipped to listen to his voice. Jesus promised that his message would resound in us through the Holy Spirit: "The Advocate, the holy Spirit that the Father will send in my name — he will teach you everything and remind you of all that [I] told you" (Jn 14:26). The same Holy Spirit who inspired the writing of Scripture is given to us to guide our reading of Scripture. It is through the Holy Spirit that the words of Scripture come alive when we read them.

> The same Holy Spirit who inspired the writing of Scripture is given to us to guide our reading of Scripture.

Like any gift of the Holy Spirit, the graces we need to read Scripture properly are given in response to prayer. If we want the help of the Holy Spirit, we should ask for it. He can certainly help us on those days when we forget to ask (fortunately he does), but it should be our practice to begin our every time of Scripture reading with a prayer. It can be a simple "Holy Spirit, inspire and guide me as I read the Bible today." Or it could be the prayer to the Holy Spirit, the *Come, Holy Spirit.* What is important is that we express our dependence on the Holy Spirit to guide us, acknowledging our need for help in order to read Scripture as God's word.

> To arrive at a completely valid interpretation of words inspired by the Holy Spirit, one must first be guided by the Holy Spirit and it is necessary to pray for that, to pray much, to ask in prayer for the interior light of the Spirit and docilely accept the light, to ask for the love that alone enables one to understand the language of God who "is love" (1 Jn 4:8, 16). While engaged in the very work of interpretation [of Scripture], once must remain in the presence of God as much as possible.
>
> — POPE JOHN PAUL II, ADDRESS OF APRIL 23, 1993,
> ON THE INTERPRETATION OF THE BIBLE IN THE CHURCH

How does the Holy Spirit help us read Scripture? What do his gifts and graces do within us? From my own experience of reading Scripture, I believe I can pick out four ways the Holy Spirit helps me.

First, *the Holy Spirit guides us to have a correct understanding of the inspired meaning of the words of Scripture.* This is not an infused grace of enlightenment that strikes us while we are passively staring into space; it is a work of the Spirit that cooperates with our own hard work in trying to understand a biblical text. It can begin with the simple grace of a clear mind. Some days I am so tired or preoccupied that I have a hard time reading even a newspaper with much understanding. I read through some news item, perhaps on the state of the economy, and at the end have no clear idea what I read. Sometimes, I am similarly afflicted when I turn to the Bible. I read a passage, but the words seem to bounce off my mind like hail off a roof.

Reading Scripture with proper attention demands that we do it when our minds are alert. This means making a conscious effort to set aside distractions, of course. But I also think that a clear mind is a grace of the Holy Spirit; Scripture passages only come alive for me when I am able to pay attention to what they are saying. I try to read carefully, understanding what I am reading. I believe that the Holy Spirit enters into this process by guiding my efforts.

Sometimes, I receive insights into a passage that seem to come out of the blue, and it is easy to acknowledge them as insights from the Spirit in response to my prayer for understanding. But most often, his grace works in a very gentle and unobtrusive manner, guiding my efforts rather than replacing them. However the Holy Spirit works, the end result is what is important. Our aim should be to have a correct understanding of the inspired meaning of the words of Scripture. When we have finished reading, we should have a sense that we basically understand what we read.

Second, *the Holy Spirit enables us to read the Bible as God's word to us*, a message addressed to us as individuals with meaning for today. Often after studying a passage of Scripture, I will have the sense that I understand it, particularly if I have made use of study aids. But other times, I will feel that something important is missing: the meaning of the passage for me. I may understand the passage but not grasp its point for my life.

For example, in studying the Gospel of John some years ago, I learned many things about the episode of the woman caught in the act of adultery (Jn 8:1-11). I found out that scholars agree that this passage was written by someone other than John and that it was a late addition to the Gospel. In reading the passage, I noticed what might have been a double standard: why wasn't the man who was caught in the same sin also hauled before Jesus, since the law prescribed the same penalty for him? I turned to the Old Testament laws on adultery and read them as background. I noted the self-righteousness of the scribes and

Pharisees, and that their real intent was to put Jesus on the spot rather than to uphold the law. I found out that scholars don't know what Jesus wrote on the ground; they don't even have any theories that struck me as likely.

I noted many other details about the passage, and I was able to recreate the episode quite vividly in my imagination. But I still had little sense of what the message of the passage was for *me*. If this event had been omitted from the Bible, my own spiritual life would have been little poorer at this point.

It was only after prayer and further reflection that some messages for me began to emerge. I began to see that in my own relationship with Jesus, I stood in the place of the woman: I have sinned. Jesus does not pretend that I am not a sinner, just as he did not tell the woman that it was okay for her to commit adultery. But neither does Jesus look on my sin as an opportunity he had been waiting for to condemn me. There is a sadness in his eyes that I have sinned, but also a gentleness. There is a message for me in his words, "Do not sin any more" (Jn 8:11).

It is one thing to read Jn 15:16 and understand that Jesus is telling his disciples that he had chosen them; it is another thing to hear those words spoken to oneself: "It was not you who chose me, but I who chose you."

Another message for me also came through this passage. In my dealings with my children, I saw myself acting like the scribes and Pharisees. How often did I uphold the law primarily out of self-righteousness rather than out of concern for them? How often was I harsh and inconsiderate of their feelings, even when their conduct called for correction? How often was I quick to condemn, failing to give them the patient attention that would help them grow into maturity?

Sometimes, the word of God from Scripture that is addressed to me does not come by way of example, as in this case, but by a more direct word. It is one thing to read Jn 15:16 and understand that Jesus is telling his disciples that he had chosen them; it is another thing to hear those words spoken to oneself: "It was not you who chose me, but I who chose you."

If the words of Scripture are to come alive to us as a here-and-now communication from God, then the Holy Spirit must bring those words to life, transforming them from squiggles of ink on a page to words spoken now, addressed to us by name. If what we read is to transform us, then the transforming power of the Spirit must be at work within us, for only the Spirit has the power to give life and growth.

Third, *the Holy Spirit gives us insight into the mysteries of God that Scripture reveals.* In the words of the Second Vatican Council, "Through divine revelation, God chose to show forth and communicate himself" (*Divine Revelation*, no. 6). Scripture does not merely contain facts about God; Scripture is the vehicle of God's revelation of himself.

> The Holy Spirit can cause words of Scripture that we have read many times to suddenly stun us with the truths they reveal about God.

Again, an example might help. The opening verses of John's Gospel address great mysteries: that the Word existed from eternity and is God, that all things were created through the Word, that the Word became flesh and lived among us. If John's words do not arouse profound wonder and awe in us, then we are only skimming the surface of their meaning. These words should lead us into contemplation of the mysteries of God and of the Incarnation. Yet our limited human understanding is woefully inadequate in the face of the mysteries of God. Now we can see only a dim reflection of God, as if in a clouded mirror (see 1 Cor 13:12). But the Holy Spirit can give us glimpses of the reality of God. The Holy Spirit can cause words of Scripture that we have read many times to suddenly stun us with the truths they reveal about God.

Such graces cannot be forced; they can only be prayed for and gratefully received. We can ask the Spirit to remove the "veil" in our minds as we read Scripture so that in the words of the Bible we encounter the one who speaks through them. We can ask that God's word to us be a revelation of himself. We can ask that we receive the grace of being drawn up into the mysteries of God, the gift of a fleeting glimpse of his face.

Fourth, *the Holy Spirit inspires our response to God in prayer.* He moves our wills to embrace what we read, and he moves our hearts to respond in joy. He gives us words to express our response — and the wordless sense of God's presence. If our reading of Scripture is truly an encounter with the God who reveals himself through its words, then our response, naturally and inevitably, has to be prayer. And, as we discover, prayer that is not graced by the Holy Spirit can be dry and difficult. Hence, we need the help of the Spirit if we are to respond as we should to the word we read.

> We need the help of the Spirit if we are to respond as we should to the word we read.

The Holy Spirit can work in us in very quiet ways. When I first began to read the Bible in a daily and serious way many years ago, I began each reading with a brief prayer that the Lord would speak to me through the words that I read. It was a simple, informal prayer, but a prayer that I never omitted. At first, my reading of Scripture was merely interesting; it had a freshness because I had never read the Bible before and was reading many passages for the first time. But one day, after months of daily reading, I became aware that I was reading Scripture on a different level than when I began. I was reading it as God's word to me, not merely as an interesting book. I became aware that, in my reading, the Lord was speaking to me — about himself, about me, and about my life with him.

I realized then that my prayer was being answered, that the Lord was speaking to me as I read. I also realized that he had been doing this for some time. His speaking to me through the words of Scripture had come so gently that I hadn't immediately been aware of what was happening. He had not answered my prayer by a voice, abruptly thundering from the heavens; he had answered it by gradual degrees, quietly, peacefully. If I had been more alert, I would no doubt have noticed it sooner.

What I experienced then was the work of the Holy Spirit within me. It was not simply an emotion; it was not a startling revelation; it was rarely dramatic. But my heart did burn within me as I read the words of Scripture, and I read even familiar passages with new understanding and insight into their meaning for me. I had begun reading Scripture because I knew it was a good thing to do; now I read eagerly, with a hunger and thirst for the word of God. I experienced what I read as God's words addressed to me, speaking to my daily experience of following Christ.

Faithful to the promise of Jesus, the Holy Spirit will be with us if we ask, and will assist us to read Scripture as the word of God

To me, this grace was given gradually. Others have experienced more sudden and dramatic workings of the Holy Spirit within them, drawing them to the pages of Scripture with an overwhelming attraction, making the words of Scripture come alive to them as never before. The very suddenness with which this gift can be given testifies to the power of the Holy Spirit. It is he who makes the words come alive; it is he who inflames our hearts with eagerness to read and embrace what we read; it is he who enlightens our minds so that we understand what we read.

This work of the Holy Spirit is a gift. Our part is to be faithful in our reading, serious in our study, and prayerful in seeking the inspiration of the Holy Spirit. The rest is up to him, and we can rely on him to do his part. He may act gradually or dramatically. But, faithful to the promise of Jesus, the Holy Spirit will be with us if we ask, and will assist us to read Scripture as the word of God:

> "If you then, who are wicked, know how to give good gifts
> to your children, how much more will the Father in heaven
> give the holy Spirit to those who ask him?"

> — Lk 11:13

Words of Life

> Then he said to all, "If anyone wishes to come after me,
> he must deny himself and take up his cross daily and fol-
> low me. For whoever wishes to save his life will lose it, but
> whoever loses his life for my sake will save it. What profit
> is there for one to gain the whole world yet lose or forfeit
> himself?"
>
> — Lk 9:23-25

We can read these words of Jesus in a variety of ways. We can read them in a very general and impersonal sense, as a law of cause and effect: if anyone does this, then that happens. We can understand what the words mean and nod agreement, much as we would to the sentence, "If anyone drops a rubber ball on a concrete driveway, it will bounce." However, this kind of reading would give these words of Jesus no more meaning for our lives than the words about the bouncing properties of a rubber ball.

These words can also be understood as a command: "You must deny yourself and take up a cross." We can even acknowledge that we are to obey this command, along with many other commands and laws: "You must pay your income taxes by April 15 of each year." While this brings the words of Jesus one step closer to us, we are still not truly hearing those words as his words to us. Reading the Bible merely as a book of dos and don'ts is not reading Scripture as the word of God.

We can, finally, read these words as the word of God to us and for us, a personal rather than impersonal command. We might read them as if they were addressed to us by name:

> Then he said to George Martin, "If you want to be my fol-
> lower, renounce yourself and your own desires, take up
> your cross every day and follow me. If you try to preserve
> your life, you will lose it. But if you expend your life for my
> sake, without worrying about yourself, then you will find

true life. What gain would it be for you, George, to become wealthy and free of responsibilities, but to ruin yourself in the process?"

To listen to the words of Scripture as God speaking to us, we must listen to them in the concrete situations of our lives. To take up our cross and follow Jesus isn't just a nice general metaphor; it refers to following the path for our lives that Jesus reveals to us and asks of us, and bearing whatever difficulties and sacrifices that path entails. It means not letting the trials and difficulties make us turn back from the way that Jesus wants us to walk.

> To listen to the words of Scripture as God speaking to us, we must listen to them in the concrete situations of our lives.

Since each of our life situations is different, the specific meaning of these words of Jesus will be different for each of us. We may be facing a choice of taking one job rather than another, knowing that the lower-paying job would be of greater service to other people and to God. We may have the opportunity to move to a better climate, but have retired parents dependent upon us where we are living now. We may have the opportunity to become a caregiver — taking a physically or mentally disabled relative into our house — but realize that this would call for great sacrifice.

In most cases, taking one course rather than another would not be a matter of sin. But it is often clear which course best represents following after Jesus and imitating him as a servant. In these situations, our reading of Scripture will let God speak to us and our concrete situation in very specific terms. God's words to us then will not be merely abstract truths or general commands. They will be words of strength and consolation for the specific choice we make: "Whoever loses his or her life for my sake, by providing a home for one of my sisters or brothers who needs it, will find abundant life." They will be words of promise, specifically addressed to us: "If you choose now not the easier path, but the more difficult path that I am calling you to follow, you will have chosen the way that is best for you." They will be words that put our life and choices in perspective: "What gain is it for you to have everything the way you want it, but to have forsaken my path and my calling?"

Music exists only in the performance and hearing. So, too God's word only truly exists as it is addressed to us and listened to by us.

A woman who was deaf from birth might find the musical score to a Beethoven symphony in the library and become fascinated by it. She could spend hours studying it, even memorizing the way the written notes followed one upon the other. But because of her deafness, she would never truly experience and understand the greatness of Beethoven's symphony. For Beethoven did not primarily write notes; he created music, a living reality only dimly captured in the written score. Music exists only in the performance and hearing. So, too, God's word only truly exists as it is addressed to us and listened to by us. The words of Scripture must be played out in our lives, as it were, brought to life as music is brought to life in a performance.

We should pray that the Holy Spirit be active in us, prompting us to read the words of Scripture with reverence, giving us wisdom and insight to understand them, guiding us in applying them to our own lives, strengthening us to gladly respond in faith and obedience. We should have confidence that in answer to our prayer, he will speak not only to our minds, but also to our hearts.

For Christians, it is an article of faith that the Bible conveys God's revelation of himself; for one who reads the Bible as the word of God, it is a matter of experience. Those who read the words of Scripture under the guidance and inspiration of the Holy Spirit can truly experience that God does speak to them, addressing them by name.

Resources

The indispensable resources for hearing the word of God are your own ears and mind and heart; no one can listen to God for you. Some auxiliary materials may, however, help stimulate reflection and listening. The following are, again, only a smattering:

Some Scripture reading aids include questions for reflection, to help apply what is read to oneself:

- *God's Word Today* magazine includes a reflection question for every daily reading.
- My *Bringing the Gospel of Matthew to Life* and *Bringing the Gospel of Mark to Life* (available from amazon.com) have reflection questions every two or three verses.

Some books of meditations on Scripture passages can stimulate one's own reflections:

- My *Meeting Jesus in the Gospels* (Servant Books) is a series of short reflections on Gospel passages
- The Word Among Us Press publishes a number of meditative and devotional books with a biblical focus: http://bookstore.wau.org or call 1-800-775-9673 for a catalogue.

Study Guide

1. Have I ever experienced my heart burning within me when I read Scripture or heard it proclaimed from the pulpit? If so, what was the impact of this experience on my life?

2. The fundamental attitude that we should bring to Scripture is an open heart: an eagerness to listen to the word of God and a willingness to heed it. To what extent is this my attitude when I sit down to read the Bible?

3. Do I believe that God really does want to speak to me through his word in Scripture? What does his wanting to speak to me say about my value in his eyes?

4. "What I am reading is written to me." Was this my attitude the last time I read a passage from the Bible? Did what I read apply to me as if it had been written particularly to and for me?

5. "What I am reading is written about me." Do I identify in a special way with any of the people I read about in Scripture? Am I able to take what happened to them as a lesson and example for me?

6. To what extent have I already experienced God speaking to me through the words of Scripture? Have I ever had an experience like St. Augustine's, when a particular Scripture passage bore personal meaning for me?

7. What is God saying to me now — or what has he said to me recently — through the words of Scripture?

8. Am I aware of the activity of the Holy Spirit in my life? How have I experienced his graces and promptings? How often do I pray to the Holy Spirit for guidance?

9. In the section on the Holy Spirit, four ways are suggested in which the Holy Spirit aids us in our Scripture reading. In which of these ways has the Holy Spirit helped me to read Scripture as God's word to me?

10. Has the Bible become words of life for me, or is it simply a book I find interesting?

11. Do I yearn for, and pray for, God to speak words of life to me?

FOUR

Praying

When the angels went away from them to heaven, the shep-
herds said to one another, "Let us go, then, to Bethlehem to
see this thing that has taken place, which the Lord has made
known to us." So they went in haste and found Mary and
Joseph, and the infant lying in the manger. When they saw
this, they made known the message that had been told them
about this child. All who heard it were amazed by what had
been told them by the shepherds. And Mary kept all these
things, reflecting on them in her heart.

— Lk 2:15-19

The events surrounding the birth of Jesus were not so simple as our Christmas cribs may lull us into thinking. Because we are so familiar with the Christmas story, we may think that we un-derstand all there is to understand about Jesus' birth. But if we read the opening chapters of the Gospels of Matthew and Luke slowly and thoughtfully, we will find much to reflect on.

What great faith was required of Joseph! What thoughts must have run through his mind! He knew Mary to be a very good and devout young woman. But when "she was found with child through the holy Spirit" (Mt 1:18), what great grace he must have received to accept that God had chosen the woman that he had chosen, and that her pregnancy was God's doing. The angel's assurance that she had conceived through the Holy Spirit (Mt 1:20) raised more questions than it answered, for who could understand how God would "save his people from their sins" (Mt 1:21) through a child born to a peasant couple living in a small village?

An angel appeared in "the glory of the Lord" and announced to startled shepherds that "today in the city of David a savior has been born for you who is Messiah and Lord" (Lk 2:9, 11). The Messiah was expected to be a king who would free God's people from Roman rule and usher in a golden age. Yet the shepherds are told that they would find the Messiah "wrapped in swaddling clothes and lying in a manger" (Lk 2:12). How could one who is Messiah and Lord be born in such humble circumstances that his parents had to use a manger — an animal feeding trough — as a makeshift cradle? There seems to be a radical disconnect between a heavenly messenger clothed in the glory of God and a message about a child born in poverty.

> Reading Scripture can play an important part in coming into his presence and listening to him. For many of us, reading Scripture each day will be the best springboard to prayer that we have available.

"And Mary kept all these things, reflecting on them in her heart" (Lk 2:19). It would have been difficult for her to fully comprehend all that was happening. She knew that God was at work in her and that what was happening was part of his plan. But to know that God's hand is guiding us isn't the same as understanding all that he is doing. Mary's faith and her willingness to be "the handmaid of the Lord" (Lk 1:38) never faltered. Still, she had to reflect on the events surrounding her Son's birth, pondering them in her heart. Her heartfelt pondering provides a model for us in our prayerful use of Scripture.

We may think of prayer as words we say, whether they be the set prayers that we learned as children or the informal prayers that come from our heart. Words are indeed one aspect of our prayer, but they must be based on and a result of a more fundamental contact with God. In ordinary life, we speak with a friend face-to-face. So, too, in our conversation with God: we must be in his presence, listening to him as well as speaking to him, if we are to pray properly. Reading Scripture can play an important part in coming into his presence and listening to him. For many of us, reading Scripture each day will be the best springboard to prayer that we have available. Mary provides us with a model for how we should ponder in our hearts what we read in Scripture.

Mary was present at the wedding feast at Cana when Jesus worked his first miracle (Jn 2:1-11). She was present by the cross (Jn 19:25-27). She was present when the Holy Spirit fell on those assembled in the upper room on Pentecost (Acts 1:13-14; 2:1-4). She was not called to publicly proclaim the good news, nor to heal the sick or work wonders. Her call was to be present, and to treasure the events of Jesus' life in her heart. Even when the actions of Jesus baffled her or caused her pain, as they did when he stayed behind in Jerusalem at the age of twelve (Lk 2:41-50), she "kept all these things in her heart" (Lk 2:51).

> Our reading, our study, and especially our listening to the word of God as it speaks to us through Scripture, give us a treasure that we can hold in our hearts.

Being in the presence of the Lord and treasuring his words in our hearts is the first step of prayer. It is also the first fruit of our reading Scripture: we are simply there, as it was, while the saving plan of God unfolds through Abraham and Moses and the prophets, and finally through Jesus. Our reading, our study, and especially our listening to the word of God as it speaks to us through Scripture, give us a treasure that we can hold in our hearts.

In pondering the events of Jesus' life, Mary was not merely thinking them over. We think things over when we are detached from them and they don't affect us very much. Still less did she brood over what was happening, as we can find ourselves doing when our lives don't seem to be going the way we feel they should. Mary's pondering was her meditation on events that affected her deeply, a faith-filled meditation that recognized that the hand of God was present in every situation, even when she did not fully understand God's plan. She knew that what was happening was happening because of God's love for his people and for her, and in her heart she both treasured that love and returned it. Her meditation was her attempt to more fully enter into the mystery that she had been called to live.

Just as Mary "kept all these things, reflecting on them in her heart" (Lk 2:19), so we are called to keep the word of God that has been addressed to us.

The First Steps

Jesus said, "Whoever loves me will keep my word, and my Father will love him, and we will come to him and make our dwelling with him" (Jn 14:23). We might understand this verse to be a repetition of an earlier verse: "If you love me, you will keep my commandments" (Jn 14:15). Doing what Jesus commands is certainly a part of keeping the word of Jesus. However, there is also a deeper meaning to what Jesus asks when he says, "keep my word." Keeping his word means listening for his word, desiring to be formed by his word, constantly meditating on his word, keeping his word in our hearts and minds. Those who keep the word of Jesus let it penetrate into them and transform them.

> Keeping the word of God in our hearts, making the word of God our home, letting the word of God penetrate into us — this is the first step of prayer.

Jesus promised those who believed in him, "If you remain in my word, you will truly be my disciples" (Jn 8:31). The word translated as "remain" can also be translated as "stay" or "abide." It suggests the image of living in the word of Jesus as we live in our family home, a place of security that we can always return to, a place where we are loved. The image of God's word as our home carries notions of intimacy and familiarity. To keep Jesus' word is to abide in his word as our place of rootedness in the world.

Keeping the word of God in our hearts, making the word of God our home, letting the word of God penetrate into us — this is the first step of prayer. The transition from reading and listening to praying isn't an abrupt one. As we read with reverence the words of the Bible, we in fact begin to pray. When we read a psalm properly, we pray it as a prayer. When we marvel at God's love for us, treasuring it in our hearts, our attitude is like that of Paul exclaiming, "Oh, the depth of the riches and wisdom and knowledge of God!" (Rom 11:33), an exclamation that is a prayer.

The Second Vatican Council taught that prayer should complement our reading of Scripture, so that we enter into a dialogue with God. We listen to him when we read Scripture, and we respond to him in prayer. Our prayer is our conversation with God, using our own words or the words of Scripture to express the thoughts of our hearts.

> Prayer should accompany the reading of Sacred Scripture, so that God and man may talk together; for "we speak to Him when we pray; we hear Him when we read the divine saying" (St. Ambrose).
>
> — *DIVINE REVELATION*, NO. 25

Besides the time we spend reading Scripture, then, we need to take time for personal prayer, our communication with God. Many people — myself included — like to set aside time for prayer immediately after their time for Scripture reading, so that the word they have heard in their reading can become the basis for their conversation with God. Others prefer to separate reading and prayer times. But however they are scheduled, it is important that we allow times for both reading and prayer. We shouldn't skimp on one for the sake of the other. Just as we need to spend a certain amount of time each day with the Bible in order to make reading it a part of our lives, so we will need to take steps in order to keep the word of God in our hearts and respond in prayer.

Our prayer might begin by asking for the assistance of the Holy Spirit as we pray, since the Holy Spirit comes to our aid when we do not know how to pray (Rom 8:26-27).

> In the same way, the Spirit too comes to the aid of our weakness; for we do not know how to pray as we ought, but the Spirit itself intercedes with inexpressible groanings. And the one who searches hearts knows what is the intention of the Spirit, because it intercedes for the holy ones according to God's will.
>
> — Rom 8:26-27

We should make an effort to place ourselves and ask the Spirit to place us in the presence of God. If we must be alone with God to listen to him speaking to us through the words of Scripture, we must also be alone with him in order to respond to his speaking with our prayer. Being alone with God does not mean ignoring our problems or trying by sheer willpower to put preoccupations out of our minds. It means bringing them to God, laying them at his feet, and letting go of them. Our focus must be on him, not on our problems or distractions. If we do this, we may be able to view our problems through his perspective.

Nor does being alone with God mean that we must shut ourselves off from other people. We can be in his presence while praying in the midst of a group of people; on the other hand, we can be shut in our closet and have our minds far from him. To be alone with God means to put ourselves fully in his presence, whether we are praying by ourselves or with others.

Thus, our initial prayer should be a prayer that we can truly be in God's presence. It should be a prayer that the Holy Spirit will draw us into being alone with God, attentive to his word, able to respond with love to the love that he has for us. We shouldn't demand of ourselves that we achieve some instant mystical state, but neither should we neglect this prayer; it is better to spend a few extra minutes in preparation than to rush into our prayer time with distractions in the forefront of our minds.

Praying the Words of Scripture

One way our prayer can be enriched by Scripture is to pray the prayers that are in the Bible, incorporating them into our prayer life.

When the apostles asked Jesus to teach them how to pray, he taught them the prayer that we know as the Our Father (Lk 11:1-4; see also Mt 6:9-13). We are so familiar with this prayer that we often say it without thinking about what we are saying and without fully meaning what we pray. It is very worthwhile to make the Our Father a text that we meditate on periodically, dwelling on the meaning of every word and then praying it slowly and consciously. Even the first two words — *Our Father* — are so full of meaning that they could be the basis of much reflection and conversation with God.

One way our prayer can be enriched by Scripture is to pray the prayers that are in the Bible, incorporating them into our prayer life.

But the Our Father isn't the only prayer in the New Testament. The book of Revelation contains prayers offered by the saints and angels in John's vision of heaven. They express the inestimable majesty of God, and are prayers of profound adoration and praise:

> "Holy, holy, holy is the Lord God almighty,
>   who was, and who is, and who is to come."

>   — Rev 4:8

Some of Paul's letters include hymns that were sung in the early Church; Philippians 2:6-11 is one such hymn, and Colossians 1:15-20 is another.

The Old Testament contains many prayers. The song of victory after passing through the Red Sea (Ex 15:1-18) is the first of many canticles sung to express the glory of God and to thank him for his saving acts. These prayers are scattered throughout the books of the Old Testament; some editions of the Bible print them in a distinctive format to make it apparent that they are hymns.

But above all, the prayers of the Bible are the Psalms. They grew out of the life of worship of God's people; many of them were composed to be sung in the Temple. They were written over the course of centuries. Some are hymns of praise; some thank God for deliverance from enemies. Others are prayers of desolation, begging God for deliverance, wondering how long it will be before he intervenes to rescue his people. They were originally meant to be sung; we no longer possess the music and have them only in the form of poetry.

> We should make an effort to make the Psalms our prayers. They are inspired prayers — inspired by the Holy Spirit, who is the necessary inspiration for all prayer.

The Psalms were prayers that Jesus and his followers prayed. At the end of his last supper with his disciples, "after singing a hymn, they went out to the Mount of Olives" (Mk 14:26). The "hymn" was likely Psalms 114-118, sung at the end of a Passover meal.

The Psalms were the prayers of the early Church. In the letters of the New Testament, we find the exhortations, "Be filled with the Spirit, addressing one another [in] psalms and hymns and spiritual songs, singing and playing to the Lord in your hearts" (Eph 5:18-19), and "Let the word of Christ dwell in you richly, as in all wisdom you teach and admonish one another, singing psalms, hymns, and spiritual songs with gratitude in your hearts to God" (Col 3:16).

We should make an effort to make the Psalms our prayers. They are inspired prayers — inspired by the Holy Spirit, who is the necessary inspiration for all prayer. They have been the prayers of the Church since the time of Jesus.

We may find some of the Psalms difficult to pray. Some express sentiments that we would hesitate to make our own, especially self-righteousness and contempt for enemies. It's doubtful that many of us could simply pray, "May God rain burning coals upon them, / cast them into the grave never more to rise" (Ps 140:11) or "Happy those who seize your children / and smash them against a rock" (Ps 137:9). While these are extreme examples, it is certain that some of the Psalms are less likely to express the thoughts of our hearts than others.

The important thing is that many of the Psalms do express very well what we want to express in our prayer. The first time I prayed my way through the 150 Psalms, I marked the ones that readily appealed to me, and found I had checked slightly over half of them. Later, I grew to like some of those I didn't check that first time through. To be sure, I don't find that each psalm that I like expresses my every mood in prayer. Some of the Psalms are most appropriate for confession of sin and asking of forgiveness; Psalm 51 is my favorite of these. Other psalms are better for expressing our praise, and still others our cry for help. If our prayer has its seasons, there is likely a psalm suited to its every mood.

The first step in praying the Psalms is to become familiar with them and grow in our understanding of each of them. We should initially read them and study them as we would any other part of Scripture. They should be read as poems, for they are poetry. We may want to try different translations of the Psalms to see which we like best. Once we are familiar with the Psalms and have a basic understanding of them, we can begin using them in our prayer. Perhaps we will want to begin our prayer time by reciting a psalm; perhaps we will prefer to have a storehouse of favorite psalms to end our prayers with, drawing upon the one that best sums up and expresses the way our prayer has gone that day. Here the great variety to be found in the Psalms works to our benefit.

Using Scripture as a Springboard to Prayer

There are many ways of basing our prayer on our Scripture reading, although they all accomplish the same purpose and have many features in common.

The simplest approach is to read a passage from the Bible, then upon it, and enter into a conversation with the Lord based on our reading and reflection (Some of us find it most natural to pray to God, or to our Father; others to pray to Jesus. I will therefore speak of praying to "the Lord," allowing you understand the Lord to be either God the Father or Jesus). The reading might be a passage from that day's regular Scripture reading, particularly if we are reading from the New Testament. Or it might be specially chosen for prayer — perhaps from the Gospels — if our regular reading is from a book of Scripture that we find difficult to use as the basis of prayer (it isn't easy to pray a genealogy in the book of Numbers!).

> The simplest approach is to read a passage from the Bible, then reflect upon it, and enter into a conversation with the Lord based on our reading and reflection.

The amount we read should not be great. After carefully reading the passage we have chosen, we reflect on it, savor it, absorb it into our minds and hearts, and listen to what the Lord may be saying to us through it. This then can be the subject matter of our prayer, our conversation with the Lord. I will say more about the conversational aspect of our prayer a little later.

Another approach is to make reading itself our prayer, our conversation with the Lord. This calls for a very slow reading that allows us to linger over every verse, even over individual words. We read a verse, reflect on it, listen to God speaking to us through it, and respond to him from our hearts. We only move on to the next verse when we have extracted all the meaning that we can from the first, turning it over in our hearts in the presence of the Lord, talking it over with him in prayer.

With this approach, there will be no set amount that we plan to read. If we are reading a passage that does not speak very forcefully to our hearts, we may find that at the end of our prayer time we have covered a sizeable amount of Scripture, because none of it provided us with very much material for reflection and prayer that day. On other days, we may find that our entire prayer time is taken up with reflecting on a single verse and praying through all the insights we receive from it.

Whichever approach we use, we should keep in mind that our goal is to have a good conversation with the Lord. We are not trying to cover a certain amount of Scripture; we are not trying to compose an eloquent prayer that might be printed in a prayer book some day. We will have good days and bad days; we will experience dryness and frustration but also experience the presence of the Lord, touching our hearts. What is important is our faithfulness, our attitude of heart in turning toward him, our opening of ourselves to the power of the Holy Spirit. Beyond that, the insights we receive and the depths of prayer that we experience are gifts of the Holy Spirit, subject to his control, not ours.

> After carefully reading the passage we have chosen, we reflect on it, savor it, absorb it into our minds and hearts, and listen to what the Lord may be saying to us through it. This then can be the subject matter of our prayer, our conversation with the Lord.

The approach that I use most often in praying from the Scripture combines the two approaches described above. I usually base my prayer on the passage that I am reading for that day from whatever book of Scripture that I am working my way through. As I read during my regular reading time, I mark in the margin any verses that strike me as likely to provide food for reflection and application to my own life. Should any verse immediately speak to me as if it were the Lord speaking to me, of course, I mark it (and sometimes go immediately to prayer, preferring to finish up my regular reading later on).

When I have finished my set reading, I turn to prayer and go back over the verses I've marked, one by one, using them as material for reflection. I listen to what the Lord may wish to say to me through them and make that the basis of my prayer. My experience is that there is usually something, even in the driest passages of Scripture, that will strike my mind in a fresh way and provide food for prayer. If one marked passage doesn't provide enough basis for prayer, I turn to another one. Sometimes, though, the first passage provides ample material for my prayer time, as I trace and retrace its message and implication for me, as I apply it to my life, as I let it sink into my heart as the word of God.

There is one potential pitfall in praying with Scripture: our prayer time might become merely a time of Scripture reading. Our reading and study of Scripture should never replace our turning to the Lord in prayer and conversing with him. If we find we are spending more and more of our prayer time reading Scripture, we should take appropriate means to restore the balance. Perhaps the Lord does want us to read Scripture more, but he most likely doesn't want that additional reading to be done at the expense of our prayer.

It is important, then, that our reading lead into prayer or become prayer. We read about God or Jesus in Scripture as a *him*; we address him in our prayers as a *you*. We do not merely read *about* him; we converse *with* him, one person to another. St. Teresa of Ávila considered prayer to be simply a heart-to-heart conversation with him who loves us.

Our reading and reflecting has provided us with the subject matter of our conversation with the Lord. If we read the parable of the Prodigal Son, our prayer that day could focus on our own need to continually return to the Lord to receive his forgiveness. We could express to the Lord our desire to love him and our sorrow at not loving him perfectly. We could ask him for the strength to make a new start. We could express gratitude that our Father does search the horizon for us, waiting for us to return home. We could rejoice that he would throw a party to welcome us home, and that he did not hesitate to send his own Son so that we might have forgiveness and life.

> Mental prayer is nothing else than an intimate friendship, a frequent heart-to-heart conversation with Him by whom we know ourselves to be loved.
>
> — St. Teresa of Ávila, *Life*, ch. 8

The Scripture that we read, the inspirations that we are given by the Holy Spirit, and our own needs will determine the type of prayer conversation we will have. Some passages lend themselves most to rejoicing in the Lord's love, thanking him for it. Other passages rather bluntly present the cost of discipleship, calling us to lay down our lives, and may move us to prostrate ourselves in submission to the Lord.

Whatever passage we read, the key to our conversation is given by St. Teresa: our prayer should be simple but heartfelt conversation, informal and unpretentious. It is the response we make to listening to the Lord speak to us through the words of Scripture.

Our conversation does not have to use many words, or ultimately words at all. We may be moved to burst into praise of the Lord, thanking him for his love for us, rejoicing that he is the Lord and has called us to himself, praising him simply for being himself. If we feel like singing a hymn, we shouldn't think it in any way improper to do so. We may be led by the Holy Spirit in our prayer, as he helps us express the inexpressible longings of our heart (see Rom 8:26-27).

Our conversation may equally well end in silence, in awe before the presence of the Lord, peacefully resting in his loving care for us. The saints have taught us that a high form of prayer is wordless: simply being in the presence of the Lord, inflamed by his Spirit within us. This may be an occasional experience for many of us — something that we cannot achieve by our own efforts, but must receive as a gift of the Spirit. Both shouts of praise and quietly being at the feet of Jesus are worthy forms of prayer. Jesus welcomed the shouts of the crowd, saying that if they were silenced the stones would shout out (Lk 19:40), and he welcomed Mary sitting silently at his feet, listening to his words (Lk 10:39, 42).

Lectio Divina

There is a long tradition in the Church of *lectio divina* — Latin for "sacred reading" or "holy reading." This is the practice of using Scripture as a springboard for prayer, honed as a method of prayer by generations of those who practiced it. *Lectio divina* might be thought of as a family of methods of prayer: there is no one unique way of practicing *lectio divina* but a variety of approaches that resemble each other and have the same basic goal. Each approach consists of several steps. The chapter headings of the first part of this book could serve as the four steps of a simple form of *lectio divina*: *reading, understanding, listening, praying*. Another simple three-step process would be *reading, reflecting, praying*: we read a passage from Scripture, reflect on it, and then respond to God in prayer. In practice, these steps may become interwoven and be not so much three stages as three aspects of what we do when we read Scripture to nourish our prayer.

> *Lectio divina* might be thought of as a family of methods of prayer.

Another way of thinking of the steps or aspects in the process of *lectio divina* would be as *reading, reflecting, listening, conversing.* We read Scripture, but read reflectively, pondering what is said. We listen to the Lord speak to us through the words of Scripture, applying them to our own lives. We enter into conversation with the Lord, responding with love to the love that he has for us, talking with him as we would with a friend, while at the same time giving him the reverence that he is due. Perhaps our reverence takes the form of a prayer of thanksgiving or praise; perhaps it isn't expressed in words at all, but is our silent adoration in his presence.

I urge you to become familiar with the Bible, and to have it at hand so that it can be your compass pointing out the road to follow. By reading it, you will learn to know Christ. Note what Saint Jerome said in this regard: "Ignorance of the Scriptures is ignorance of Christ." A time-honored way to study and savor the word of God is *lectio divina,* which constitutes a real and veritable spiritual journey marked out in stages. After the *lectio,* which consists of reading and rereading a passage from Sacred Scripture and taking in the main elements, we proceed to *meditatio.* This is a moment of interior reflection in which the soul turns to God and tries to understand what his word is saying to us today. Then comes *oratio,* in which we linger to talk with God directly. Finally we come to *contemplatio.* This helps us to keep our hearts attentive to the presence of Christ, whose word is "a lamp shining in a dark place, until the day dawns and the morning star rises in your hearts" (2 Pet 1:19). Reading, study, and meditation of the Word should then flow into a life of consistent fidelity to Christ and his teachings.

— POPE BENEDICT XVI, MESSAGE TO THE YOUTH OF THE WORLD
ON THE 21ST WORLD YOUTH DAY, APRIL 9, 2006

Another way in which the steps or aspects of *lectio divina* have been characterized is *reading, meditation, prayer,* and *contemplation.* Here, *meditation* would encompass reflecting on a passage of Scripture and listening to the Lord speak to us through it; *contemplation* is our silently resting in the word and the One the word reveals. Another way the method *lectio divina* is presented is as encompassing *reading, reflection, study, meditation, prayer, contemplation,* but the basic reality is the same.

The ultimate goal of prayer is union with God. We are called to mature in the image of Christ, growing daily in the life of the Holy Spirit, and expressing that life in love and service of others. Prayer based on Scripture should bear this fruit, since our reading will keep our goal ever before our eyes.

Scripture reading should keep our prayer down to earth, so that it can be truly heaven-directed.

Daily prayer based on reading Scripture as the word of God should also help us connect the lofty aim of union with God with the day-in, day-out events of our life. If we are listening correctly, we should hear God gently speak to us about the concrete concerns of life and the very specific situations in which he is calling us to love. John pointed out that if we cannot love our brother or sister whom we do see, we can scarcely claim to love God whom we cannot see (1 Jn 4:20). Scripture reading should keep our prayer down to earth, so that it can be truly heaven-directed.

At the same time, in our prayer we should confront the mystery of God and enter into ever more fully into that mystery. For the saints of the Church, the way of prayer was the way in which knowing and loving finally became the same, a preparation for that day in which they would see God face-to-face.

Paul prayed that the Christians at Ephesus would grow into a complete knowledge of God, asking:

. . . that the God of our Lord Jesus Christ, the Father of glory, may give you a spirit of wisdom and revelation resulting in knowledge of him. May the eyes of [your] hearts be enlightened, that you may know what is the hope that belongs to his call, what are the riches of glory in his inheritance among the holy ones, and what is the surpassing greatness of his power for us who believe.

— EPH 1:17-19

The role of the Holy Spirit in our coming to this knowledge and in our prayer is all important, "for the Spirit scrutinizes everything, even the depths of God" (1 Cor 2:10). The Spirit from the heart of the Father reveals the Father to us; the Spirit in us prays to the Father. The final fruit of our listening to the word of God in Scripture and our responding in prayer is this twofold activity of the Holy Spirit, bringing about our union with the Father. The way of prayer is the way to the Father.

Resources

There are a number of helpful books available on *lectio divina*. Two of them are:

Stephen J. Binz, *Conversing with God in Scripture: A Contemporary Approach to* Lectio Divina (The Word Among Us Press).

Christine Valters Paintner and Lucy Wynkoop, O.S.B., Lectio Divina: *Contemplative Awakening and Awareness* (Paulist Press).

Study Guide

1. Do I have favorite biblical scenes or events that I ponder in my heart? What insights have I received from my pondering? Did such insights provide me with a starting point for prayer?

2. Being in the presence of Jesus and treasuring his words in our hearts is the first step of prayer. Has this been true for me? How might Mary be a model for me,

showing me what it means to be present with Jesus and ponder his words in my heart?

3. Do I feel at home in the word of God? Do I feel at home in the presence of Jesus? Am I comfortable enough in his presence to be able to talk with him in prayer?

4. How do I go about entering into the presence of the Lord? In what ways is he most present to me? How do I deal with distractions during prayer?

5. What are my favorite prayers from Scripture, apart from the psalms? Do I ever meditate on their words, in order to be able to pray them better?

6. Do I use the psalms as part of my prayers? Which are my favorite psalms? Why are they my favorites?

7. Have the words of Scripture been springboards to prayer for me? Do I read a passage and then pray about it, or pray as I read? What method works best for me?

8. St. Teresa of Ávila characterized prayer simply as a heart-to-heart conversation with him who loves us. How would I characterize the way I pray?

9. What approach to *lectio divina* works best for me? How might I adjust it to make it work even better?

10. The ultimate goal of prayer is union with God. Am I consciously trying to grow in union with God? How big a role does reading Scripture play in my efforts to better know and love God?

PART II

The Word of God

FIVE

The Word of God Comes in Human Words

In the beginning was the Word,
and the Word was with God,
and the Word was God.
He was in the beginning with God.
All things came to be through him,
and without him nothing came to be....
And the Word became flesh
and made his dwelling among us.

— JN 1:1-3, 14

It is very significant that one of the persons of the Trinity is called "the Word."

A word is something that is spoken. A word communicates and builds bridges between people. When we speak, we not only convey information but reveal something of ourselves. For a person of the Trinity to be the Word means that revelation is a part of the very nature of God.

Through the Word of God, the world was created. God spoke, and all things came into being. The Word of God is a creative word, a word of love. Nothing compelled God to create the world but his love seeking expression. When God says, "I love you," the "you" comes into being.

The Word that brought the world into being became flesh in Jesus of Nazareth. The Word of God was uttered as a man.

John's Gospel does not say that the Word lived under the *appearance* of flesh; John makes the blunt statement that the Word *became* flesh.

Nor is John content to say that the Word of God became man; John states that the Word became *flesh* — a word carrying connotations of the weakness and temptation and mortality that is the lot of humankind. In Jesus of Nazareth, God did not play at becoming human, or walk the face of the earth disguised as a man. In Jesus, the Word of God became a man, became flesh and bone, became one of us.

> John's Gospel does not say that the Word lived under the *appearance* of flesh; John makes the blunt statement that the Word *became* flesh.

The Word of God became flesh, and "made his dwelling among us" (Jn 1:14). A more literal translation of John's words would be "and pitched his tent among us." The expression has a note of familiarity; it is almost as if John wrote, "The Word of God became flesh and moved in next door to us." He who created the universe walked upon our earth. He whose love brought us into being lived with us as one of us.

It would be simpler for us to understand Jesus if he had been merely a very holy man and not the Word become flesh. And, on the other hand, it would also be simpler to understand Jesus if he had not been truly human, if the Word of God had not completely become flesh. To reject the divinity of Jesus Christ is obviously an error. But to reject his humanity, to reject that the Word *became flesh*, is no less an error.

The Gospels give us many clues to the full humanity of Jesus. We read of Jesus walking from Judea to Galilee, a distance of about sixty-five miles through very hilly country. He stopped at noon at the town of Shechem, "tired from his journey" (Jn 4:6) and thirsty, and asked a Samaritan woman for a drink of water. Do we *really* believe that he was tired and thirsty? We know that a long walk would exhaust us and make us thirsty.

But do we accept that Jesus felt the same fatigue and aches that we do? Or do we unconsciously assume that he was some sort of first-century superman, gliding along a foot off the ground, never feeling the rocks of the road through his sandals?

The Word made flesh felt the same weariness and hunger and fatigue that we experience. Our faith in Jesus Christ must take his full humanity into account. If we do not understand that *the Word became flesh*, we do not understand how God sent his Word to us.

In the same way, our listening to the word of God in Scripture must take the full humanity of that word into account. Jesus is the Word of God become human; Scripture is the word of God in human words. If we only understand Scripture as the word of God, and not as the word of God spoken in human words, we will not be able to listen correctly to God speaking to us through Scripture. Conversely, if we only understand Scripture as words written by human beings, and not as also the word of God, we will likewise fail to understand it for what it is.

Muslims believe that the Koran was dictated by the angel Gabriel to Mohammed. Mormons believe that their holy writings were found written in an unknown language upon tablets of gold. For a Christian, however, the words of God come not through angels but through human beings. They do not come in a mysterious language, but in human language. The words of God have been spoken to us in human form, just as the Word of God became human.

The human origins of the Bible can be difficult for us to accept. It is much easier to imagine that an audible voice dictated the words of Scripture to secretaries who transcribed them than to accept that God chose to reveal himself through thoughts and

> If we do not understand that the *Word became flesh*, we do not understand how God sent his Word to us. In the same way, our listening to the word of God in Scripture must take the full humanity of that word into account.

words that were authentically the thoughts and words of human beings like ourselves.

Often, the biblical authors' words reflect their humanity. The books of Samuel and Kings occasionally use a vulgar expression that translations politely paraphrase. The author of 2 Maccabees edited an earlier five-volume work into the book we find in our Bibles, and he found it a laborious undertaking, a matter "of sweat and of sleepless nights" (2 Mac 2:26). Paul occasionally interrupts his train of thought with another thought and never properly finishes his sentence. The author of the book of Revelation makes grammatical mistakes, as if Greek was not his native language; the inspiration of the Holy Spirit does not extend to grammar and style. Our translations of the Bible usually smooth over infelicities in the text to make for better reading, but they thereby remove some of the reminders that the words of Scripture were written by human beings.

> The author of the book of Revelation makes grammatical mistakes, as if Greek was not his native language; the inspiration of the Holy Spirit does not extend to grammar and style.

If we don't recognize that the word of God was uttered in words of human beings, we will not be able to listen to God's word correctly. We will read the Bible as if it were a voice whispering in our ear, reciting Genesis 1:1 to Revelation 22:21 in a monotone. Instead, we must hear God's voice speaking through a chorus of human voices — voices that at times debate with one another; voices that at times speak in poetry, at other times in song; voices that speak in parables as well as recount history; voices that can be angry or consoling. We must accept that if God has chosen to speak to us in human language, then he can choose any form of human expression and writing to convey his message.

The Word in History

To understand the Bible, we must understand its origins. God chose to speak first to a particular people, a choice that gave his words a particular form. We will read Scripture with greater understanding the more we discover how Scripture was formed and shaped by the life of God's people. God chose the descendants of Abraham to be the vehicle of his voice; he chose that in the fullness of time, his Son would be a descendant of Abraham. Our understanding of Scripture must begin with Abraham.

> We will read Scripture with greater understanding the more we discover how Scripture was formed and shaped by the life of God's people.

There is something mysterious, almost scandalous, about God's choices. It is a mystery why God should have picked out a particular individual several millennia ago, asked him to leave his native land, and called him to be the father of a people (Gen 12:1-2). Yet it is with Abraham that God's revelation breaks into human history. Why this individual, and not another? Why, after centuries of silence, did God choose to speak at this time and not sooner? We cannot know. We can only know that this is how God has chosen to speak to humankind. We must respect his choice, and listen to him as he has chosen to speak to us. Revelation begins with Abraham, our father in faith (Rom 4:11-12, 16).

The LORD said to Abram: "Go forth from the land of your kinsfolk and from your father's house to a land that I will show you.

"I will make of you a great nation,
and I will bless you;
I will make your name great,
so that you will be a blessing."

— GEN 12:1-2

Centuries after God first spoke to Abram (whom he renamed Abraham — Gen 17:5), his descendants were a slave class in Egypt. They preserved memories of their ancestors, Abraham,

Isaac, and Jacob, but professed only the sketchiest faith in the one true God. Around 1250 B.C., God selected Moses, a Sinai sheepherder who had grown up in Egypt, and revealed himself to him. God's word came unexpectedly from a burning bush (Ex 3:1-10), breaking into human history once again. God entrusted Moses with the mission of freeing the Israelites from their slavery in Egypt.

If Abraham is the father of faith, Moses is the father of the Bible.

Our Scriptures have their roots in the traditions and writings that began crystallizing in the wake of Moses some three millennia ago. If Abraham is the father of faith, Moses is the father of the Bible. Moses was more than a great civil rights leader. He was the instrument for forging the Israelites into God's people, bound by a pact, or covenant, with God. The first five books of the Old Testament have that covenant as their focal point.

We will not grasp the meaning of the Old Testament unless we understand that it is a book that grew out of the life of a people. In an era before there were police departments and hospitals, social security and unemployment checks, a person's survival depended upon belonging to a family, a tribe, a people. But a people held more in common than the means of physical survival. They had a common heritage, a common body of shared experiences. When the people in question were God's people, then their heritage of memories centered on the mighty deeds that God had performed for them. As individuals, we remember back to the days of our youth; as a people, they looked back on the days of their origin.

We get to know another person both by what he or she says and does. The Israelites grew in their knowledge of God both through his words and through his actions. His revelation was contained as much in what happened to the Israelites — as a people — as in what he explicitly said to them.

A portion of the Old Testament is taken up with writings that strike us as history, but a unique kind of history. The authors were as interested in the significance of events as in the events themselves. The Exodus of the Israelites from Egypt was one of the most decisive events in the history of God's people. It freed them from slavery, constituted them as a people, and set the pattern of life that they were to follow. It was an event in which later generations saw deep significance, one that has significance even for us.

The Old Testament began as the heritage of the Israelite people, a heritage passed from parents to children. Each generation told the succeeding generation how they had come to be a people. They taught about God, and about what it meant to be a member of God's people, by recounting the events that marked their beginning. They proclaimed God's special concern for them by telling the marvelous deeds he had done on their behalf. Recounting these events was more than an abstract history lesson: it was preaching and teaching about God:

> "If your son should ask you later on, 'What does this mean?' you shall tell him, 'With a strong hand the LORD brought us out of Egypt, that place of slavery.'"
>
> — Ex 13:14

How oral tradition is handed on affects *what* is handed on. Stories tend to get remembered in set ways; a poetic form of expression is often adopted to make memorization easier. The constant telling and retelling of a story rounds off the sharp edges, like the sea tossing and washing a small rock until it is round. This influences the Bible that we read today. A portion of the Bible is a written expression of oral traditions, the written version of a message first passed on by word of mouth. This oral handing-on has shaped the words we read and the form they are presented in.

God's revelation came to his people not only through events that revealed God's action; God's words were also spoken through the prophets, people who spoke on behalf of God. The golden age of prophecy, from about 750 to 500 B.C., included the great prophets Isaiah, Jeremiah, and Ezekiel. These were the years in which Israel first teetered on the brink of conquest by foreign powers, then was repeatedly invaded and carried off into exile, and finally, was permitted to return from exile. After that, prophecy gradually died out, and a famine came to Israel: "not a famine of bread, or thirst for water, / but for hearing the word of the LORD" (Amos 8:11).

Prophets spoke God's word to his chosen people. They spoke less of the future than of the present.

Prophets spoke God's word to his chosen people. They spoke less of the future than of the present. They brought God's judgment to bear on the course that his people were taking. Their message was often the same, a call to return to God, but each prophet addressed that message in terms of a specific historical situation and specific needs.

Old Testament prophecy must be read against the background of Old Testament history. Whether the chosen people were on the brink of conquest by foreign powers or had been conquered and were in exile determined the specific word that God addressed to them through the prophets. The prophetic message before the exile was often a call to repentance, a warning that disaster would strike if they did not return to God. It was often uttered in uncompromising and even harsh terms. But God's prophetic word to his people during their exile took on a different tone. It was a word of consolation and hope, a promise of deliverance.

> Take care and be earnestly on your guard not to forget the things which your own eyes have seen, nor let them slip from your memory as long as you live, but teach them to your children and to your children's children.
>
> — DEUT 4:9

When we read the prophetic books of the Old Testament, we need to keep in mind that they contain words addressed, first of all, to people at the time of the prophet and to the specific situation they were in. Ezekiel did not utter prophecies to twenty-first-century Americans; he proclaimed God's word to sixth-century B.C. Israelites during their exile in Babylon. Because God's word was truly spoken through Ezekiel, his prophecies contain God's revelation for all time. But it was a revelation addressed to people living more than 2,500 years ago, a word of God shaped by their situation and their needs. We are privileged to eavesdrop on Ezekiel's words to the Israelites and, through them, hear the word of God addressed to us.

In the Old Testament, both history and prophecy were manifestations of God's word. History was charged with meaning, charged with the revelation of God to his people. Prophecy was rooted in history: spoken in a historical context and bringing to light the significance in God's eyes of that moment in history. The people of God were the context for the word of God to be spoken.

The Word Becomes Words

The inspiration of the Holy Spirit cannot be limited to the inspiration of the authors of the books of the Bible. The Holy Spirit guided and inspired not only writers but also the prophets, judges, and leaders of the Old Testament, and the apostles, prophets, evangelists, and teachers of the New Testament.

In fact, while Scripture describes the Holy Spirit guiding the leaders of God's people and leaders in the early Church (Num 11:16-25 and Acts 15:22-29, for example), and while it speaks of the Spirit moving prophets to speak (2 Chron 24:20 and Acts 11:28, for example), it rarely if ever describes the Holy Spirit moving or inspiring writers to write the pages of Scripture. This does not mean that the Holy Spirit did not guide the writers of Scripture, but that this inspiration must be seen within the context of the Spirit's guidance of God's people and the Church. Within this context, the Holy Spirit inspired the creation of a body of literature that expressed the religious heritage of God's people. Apart from this context, the writing of Scripture cannot be understood.

We shouldn't imagine that God's voice came to the writers of Scripture in an audible way, giving them the exact words that they were to set down in writing. A voice from the heavens would have been heard, but wouldn't necessarily have led to human understanding and receptivity to insight. Rather, the Spirit worked by inspiration — by giving insights, by endowing human beings with wisdom, by enabling them to understand the significance of God's dealings with his people, by prompting them to write.

When Paul dictated his letters, Paul knew that he was the author of the letters, as he indicates in the first verse of every letter. He probably did not feel any different when he wrote the letters that later were included in the New Testament than he did in writing letters that have been lost and are not a part of Scripture. Paul probably prayed for God's guidance when he wrote, because he was writing to answer real needs of the early Church and wanted to answer those needs correctly. He sometimes stated that he was only giving his own opinions in his letters: "Now in regard to virgins, I have no commandment from the Lord, but I give my opinion as one who by the Lord's mercy is trustworthy" (1 Cor 7:25; see also 1 Cor 7:12). Paul, then, was not attempting to write "Scripture," but to write the truth, to proclaim the Gospel, to solve practical problems.

Nonetheless, Paul was inspired by the Holy Spirit, so what he wrote could be accepted by the Church as a written part of the new covenant, or agreement, that God was making with his people. God guided Paul when he wrote — but guided him without violating his freedom to write what he wanted to write. The Holy Spirit's guidance didn't prevent Paul's personality from showing through; it didn't even prevent him from using a few expressions we might find impolite (Gal 5:12, for example).

When we turn from books that had a single author (such as a letter by Paul) to books that underwent a long process of development under various authors and editors (such as Genesis), the matter of how the Holy Spirit's inspiration worked becomes even more complex. The Spirit guided the evolution of each book and, indeed, of the entire body of literature that is the Bible.

God guided Paul when he wrote — but guided him without violating his freedom to write what he wanted to write.

Our modern concept of authorship is one of an author sitting down and writing a book. Many of the books of the Old Testament weren't written in such a simple manner. Their "authorship" may have spanned centuries and involved many individuals in different ways.

At the core of a book might have been an ancient tradition, handed down from generation to generation by word of mouth. Perhaps several slightly different oral traditions, stemming from the same event, were handed down in different geographic areas. At various points, the traditions were written down. Later, someone edited the various written traditions into one work. Out of respect for the material they were working with, editors might choose to include several slightly different traditions without rewriting them to make them agree in details. Finally, other editors might set their hands to the book, incorporating other bits of written and oral tradition and working the book into the form in which we know it today.

This extended authorship may go against our inclination of "one book, one author," but it's a very natural process when the book in question captures the religious heritage of a people that was told, written, and edited within the context of God's continuing presence to his people.

That's why if we try to read the books of the Old Testament as if they all came from the hand of one author, we will become enmeshed in endless difficulties. If we attribute authorship directly to God himself, we will have to contend with his seeming inconsistencies and lapses of style. But if we view the Old Testament as the written religious heritage of a people, as the written result of God's dealings with them, then many problems do not arise, and many questions become answerable.

> If we try to read the books of the Old Testament as if they all came from the hand of one author, we will become enmeshed in endless difficulties.

The four Gospels likewise developed in stages:

First, Jesus of Nazareth lived in our midst and taught. He relied on the spoken word, leaving behind him neither written works nor instructions to his followers to write his words down. Instead, Jesus formed a group of followers to be the nucleus of his Church and consigned his teachings to them.

After his death, and after the Holy Spirit had been poured out on the Church, his followers proclaimed both what Jesus had taught them and taught about Jesus himself. This was the *second* stage of development of the Gospels: the teachings of the early Church. At least thirty years apparently elapsed after the death of Jesus before the writing of the first Gospel. During this time, teachings of and about Jesus were handed on in the Church. The needs of the Church influenced the selection and presentation of these teachings. The early Church was not concerned with reporting the words of Jesus or retelling incidents from his life, as a newspaper reporter might; it interpreted what Jesus did and said under the guidance of the Holy Spirit, highlighting its significance.

The *third* stage of development of the Gospels occurred when the evangelists set down the Gospels in writing. The Gospel writers had a creative role to play — sifting various elements of the tradition, examining what others had already written, selecting some incidents and omitting others, giving order to the materials they selected. Their task was not a mechanical one, and they needed the inspiration of the Holy Spirit to carry it out.

> Since many have undertaken to compile a narrative of the events that have been fulfilled among us, just as those who were eyewitnesses from the beginning and ministers of the word have handed them down to us, I too have decided, after investigating everything accurately anew, to write it down in an orderly sequence for you, most excellent Theophilus, so that you may realize the certainty of the teachings you have received.
>
> — Lᴋ 1:1-4

We cannot, therefore, consider the Gospels to be stenographic records of the words Jesus spoke, nor are they biographies of Jesus as biographies are written today. Their purpose was not to provide a biographical account of a dead person but to teach Christians about the One who still lived in their midst. The early Church was less concerned to preserve the exact words of Jesus than it was to preserve and proclaim their significance. It may shock many today to realize that the Gospels don't necessarily contain the exact words Jesus spoke. They contain the message that Jesus proclaimed, but the wording was shaped by the early Church to highlight Jesus' meaning. Hence there are discrepancies in wording between the Gospels. The early Church did not have tape recorders and on-site stenographers; it did have the Holy Spirit to guarantee its faithfulness to what Jesus taught.

The Church has strongly upheld that the Gospels faithfully hand on what Jesus Christ did and taught for our salvation. The shaping of the Gospel message by its oral handing-on did not do away with its historical basis. The work of the evangelists in writing the Gospels — choosing some incidents and omitting others, combining together teachings given on different occasions, explaining the significance of what Jesus did in terms of the needs of the early Church — did not do violence to the truth of the Gospel message. The eyewitnesses and evangelists wanted to tell the truth about Jesus Christ. Through the inspiration of the Holy Spirit, they did. With that certainty we can read the Gospels as proclamations of the salvation to be found in Jesus Christ. We can read the words of Jesus in the Gospels as his words to us.

Holy Mother Church has firmly and with absolute constancy held, and continues to hold, that the four Gospels just named, whose historical character the Church unhesitatingly asserts, faithfully hand on what Jesus Christ, while living among men, really did and taught for their eternal salvation until the day He was taken up into heaven (see Acts 1:1). Indeed, after the Ascension of the Lord the Apostles handed on to their hearers what He had said and done. This they did with that clearer understanding which they enjoyed (Jn 2:22; 12:16; cf. 14:26; 16:12-13; 7:39) after they had been instructed by the glorious events of Christ's life and taught by the light of the Spirit of truth. (see Jn 14:26; 16:13). The sacred authors wrote the four Gospels, selecting some things from the many which had been handed on by word of mouth or in writing, reducing some of them to a synthesis, explaining some things in view of the situation of their churches and preserving the form of proclamation but always in such fashion that they told us the honest truth about Jesus.

— *Divine Revelation*, no. 19

How Our Bibles Came To Be

If we were to see the book of Isaiah read by Jesus in the synagogue of Nazareth (Lk 4:16-20), or the actual letters Paul sent to Corinth, they might strike us as a little odd, even apart from their being in another language. The prophecies of Isaiah would have been preserved on a long scroll. A twenty-four foot long scroll of Isaiah, copied about a century before Jesus, was found among the Dead Sea Scrolls (scrolls discovered in caves near the Dead Sea); the scroll Jesus read from would have been much like it. Isaiah's prophecies would have been written out in Hebrew consonants, without vowels. Paul's letters were written in Greek, with words run together without spacing or punctuation.

Writing was done on parchment — shaved animal skins — or on papyrus, a kind of paper. Individual sheets were attached together to form a scroll. In the Second Letter to Timothy, Paul tells Timothy, "Try to join me soon.... When you come, bring the cloak I left with Carpus in Troas, the papyrus rolls, and especially the parchments" (2 Tim 4:9, 13). Paul identifies the books he wants not by their contents but by what they are written on. Since parchment was expensive, "the parchments" Paul especially wanted brought to him were probably scrolls of the Old Testament Scriptures.

The oldest known New Testament manuscript is a fragment from the Gospel of John, copied around A.D. 135; some of Paul's letters survive in copies made around A.D. 200. The two oldest complete Bibles date from the middle of the fourth century.

Copies of the Scriptures were comparatively rare in Old Testament times and even in the time of Jesus. Few people could read or write; ordinary people listened to the Scriptures read aloud in synagogue (see Lk 4:16-20; Acts 13:14-15). Likewise in the early Church, Old Testament Scriptures — and New Testament Scriptures, as they came to be written — were read aloud when Christians came together to worship and celebrate the Lord's Supper (see Col 4:16).

It is sobering to realize that parts of the Bible go back almost 3,000 years. We no longer have the original manuscripts that the authors wrote by hand or dictated. The Dead Sea Scrolls include the oldest surviving copies of Old Testament books or portions of books, dating to the two centuries before Jesus. The oldest known New Testament manuscript is a fragment from the Gospel of John, copied around A.D. 135; some of Paul's letters survive in copies made around A.D. 200. The two oldest complete Bibles date from the middle of the fourth century; one of them is kept in the Vatican library. Many New Testament manuscripts from the third, fourth, and fifth centuries have survived. Different manuscripts often read slightly differently or omit sections that other manuscripts include. The work of making a modern translation of Scripture thus frequently includes the burden of deciding which ancient manuscripts to follow.

The books of Scripture first existed on independent books written on separate scrolls. Only gradually did the scrolls that make up the Bible come to be collected together; still later, the Scriptures began to be printed on sheets that could be bound together as a book. Nowhere in the Bible is it stated which books make up the Bible. This is a decision that was made by the Church, under the guidance of the Holy Spirit.

At the time of Jesus, different editions of the books of the Old Testament were used by the Jewish people. Jews living in Palestine read their Scriptures in Hebrew, the language that they had spoken up to the time of the exile. (At the time of Jesus, they spoke Aramaic, a closely related language; a few chapters of the Old Testament are in Aramaic.) Jews living in other parts of the world used a Greek translation of the Old Testament, since Greek was the everyday language where they lived. No definite listing of the books that did or did not belong to the Old Testament existed for the Jews until after the time of Jesus, although there was agreement on the core of the Old Testament. The Greek edition of their Scriptures contained several books that the Hebrew edition did not contain.

When the Church began, it generally used the Greek edition of the Old Testament, since it rapidly became a Gentile Church, with Greek as its most common language. The books of the New Testament were written in Greek — even Paul's letter to

Latin-speaking Rome. When the New Testament writers wanted to quote the Old Testament, they often quoted it from the Greek edition of the Old Testament.

Although there was some discussion, the Church accepted the books contained in the Greek edition of the Old Testament as the books of the Old Testament. At the time of the Protestant Reformation, some reformers termed those books that were in the Greek (but not in the Hebrew) Old Testament as "Apocryphal" — not to be treated as God's word, as were the accepted books of the Old Testament. The Council of Trent reaffirmed that these books are inspired parts of the Old Testament, and they are so read by Catholics and Orthodox today.

Over 100 books or writings appeared in the early Church, claiming to be gospels or letters or revelations written by the apostles and Paul.

The New Testament went through a similar time of evolution and selection. Over 100 books or writings appeared in the early Church, claiming to be gospels or letters or revelations written by the apostles and Paul. Out of these, those that authentically expressed the faith of the Church and provided a reliable guide for the Christian life had to be chosen. While there was amazing consensus over what was authentic and what was not, it still required the Church's discussion and decision to select the books we read today as the New Testament. I will say more about this process in chapter seven.

The table of contents of the Bible does not indicate the order in which the books of the Bible were written. It may appear to, because Genesis deals with creation and comes first, and Revelation seems to deal with the end of the world and comes last. But the actual order in which the books of the Bible were written bears little resemblance to the order in which they appear in the Bible.

In particular, we might assume that in the New Testament, the Gospels were written first; then the letters; and finally, the book of Revelation. Actually, some of Paul's letters were written before any of the Gospels, and almost all of the New Testament letters were written before the Gospel of John. Nor are Paul's letters presented in the order in which they were written. They are presented in roughly the order of their length, with the longest, Romans, first.

The way our Bibles present its books can lull us into thinking that Scriptures were written with chapter divisions — and that Jesus spoke in verses. However, as helpful as the divisions into chapters and verses may be for locating passages, they are not a part of Scripture as it was written. The Bible was first divided into chapters in the early part of the thirteenth century by Stephen Langton; division into verses was introduced by a printer, Robert Estienne, in 1551. So if we made a reference to "John 3:16" to a first-century Christian — or even a twelfth-century Christian — we would get a blank stare.

If we made a reference to "John 3:16" to a first-century Christian — or even a twelfth-century Christian — we would get a blank stare.

More importantly, the chapter and verse divisions don't always reflect a logical division of the text of Scripture. It is handy to read a chapter a day, but the thought being developed by Paul may begin in the middle of one chapter and end in the middle of the next. Our reading should be guided by the meaning found in Scripture and the natural units of thought we find there, not by divisions introduced later.

Resources

The *Catechism of the Catholic Church* addresses the stages of God's revelation and its culmination in Jesus Christ in sections 51 to 73.

A Consuming Fire by Robert Duggan (Our Sunday Visitor) offers a penetrating analysis of the Old Testament.

The Pontifical Biblical Commission's 1964 instruction *On the Historical Truth of the Gospels* presents the Catholic Church's understanding of how the Gospels came to be written and are to be interpreted. It is printed, along with a commentary on it by Joseph A. Fitzmyer, S.J., in his book, *A Christological Catechism* (Paulist Press).

Study Guide

1. Do I have a harder time accepting the full divinity of Jesus Christ or his full humanity? What does it mean for me that he was subject to all the frailties of the human condition that I am subject to?

2. Do I accept that God speaks to us in fully human words in the Bible, just as the Word became fully human in Jesus of Nazareth? What are some of the implications of this for how I go about understanding the Bible as God's word?

3. The books of the Bible were written over a period of almost a thousand years, in some cases incorporating material that had already been handed on by word of mouth. Does this have implications for how I go about understanding these books? What might be some of these implications?

4. The people of God were the context for the word of God to be spoken. How does this help me better understand the historical books of the Bible? the prophetic books?

5. Read 2 Maccabees, chapter 15, verses 37 and 38. What does verse 38 reveal about the attitude of the author? Can the Holy Spirit inspire and guide someone without that person being aware of it?

6. Does realizing that some of the biblical books were shaped by a variety of authors and editors over the course of many decades change my view of Scripture? Do I think of the Bible as the written heritage of a people or as simply a work produced by individual inspired authors? Does this distinction make any difference in how I go about reading the Bible as God's word?

7. Do I think of the Bible as a book or as an entire library of books? I expect to find many different kinds of books in a public library, from do-it-yourself manuals to novels to history books: am I surprised that the library-that-is-the-Bible also contains many different kinds of books? What does this variety imply about how I go about understanding the Bible?

8. Does learning about the process through which the Bible came to be help me understand it better? Does its long process of development say anything to me about the way God has chosen to communicate with us through Scripture?

SIX

It Is God Who Speaks

In times past, God spoke in partial and various ways to our ancestors through the prophets; in these last days, he spoke to us through a son, whom he made heir of all things and through whom he created the universe.

— HEB 1:1-2

God revealed himself to the human race, beginning with Abraham. His revelation came in varied and partial ways, not because God wished to withhold himself from us, but because human beings had to grow in their ability to hear God. All too often God spoke, but men and women did not listen; God acted, but humans failed to perceive what was happening. The words of the prophets frequently fell on deaf ears.

The voices of the Old Testament sometimes challenge one another. The almost cynical wisdom of Ecclesiastes must be heard alongside the often prosaic advice of Proverbs.

The Old Testament is the record of the various partial ways that God spoke before the time of Jesus. The voice of God comes through human voices: Moses, Isaiah, Jeremiah, the authors of the Books of Kings and Chronicles, the authors of the Psalms. God's voice must be heard through this chorus of voices, each of them conveying some aspect of God's revelation.

The voices of the Old Testament sometimes challenge one another. The almost cynical wisdom of Ecclesiastes must be heard alongside the often prosaic advice of Proverbs. Be diligent in your work, Proverbs advises, and you will be happy. It's not so simple, rejoins Ecclesiastes; much human busyness is empty. Deuteronomy's central teaching is that when Israel is faithful to God, she prospers; when she turns away from him, disasters befall her. The Books of Judges and Kings interpret Israel's history in light of this principle; God's people are defeated in battle and taken into exile because they have not been faithful to God. The same principle is applied to individuals: the just person will prosper, the unjust person will fall: "The LORD watches over the way of the just, / but the way of the wicked leads to ruin" (Ps 1:6).

But this was not always borne out in experience. Sometimes, the unjust flourished at the expense of the just, and evil seemed to prevail over good. The book of Job explores this mystery. Countering the simple notion that the just person always flourishes, the book of Job confronts the problem of unjustified suffering. Other passages in the Old Testament question whether Deuteronomy's principle always holds true: is every national downfall a sign of infidelity? Psalm 44 laments that God has allowed his people to be defeated in battle even though they had been faithful to him (Ps 44:18-20).

We might think that demanding "eye for eye, tooth for tooth" (Lev 24:20) is a harsh law of revenge. But in Old Testament times, it was a law *limiting* vengeance to the amount of injury suffered.

Through the centuries of God's "partial and various" revelation, the Israelite people were gradually able to hear his voice more clearly. Early traditions attributed to God a wrath that was visited upon children for the sins of fathers (Ex 34:7); prophets later taught that each person would be punished only for his or her own sins (Jer 31:29-30; Ezek 33:12-20).

We must respect God's partial revelations even if they are not his final word. For example, we might think that demanding "eye for eye, tooth for tooth" (Lev 24:20) is a harsh law of revenge. But in Old Testament times, it was a law *limiting* vengeance to the amount of injury suffered. In Genesis, Lamech boasted, "I have killed a man for wounding me, / a boy for bruising me. / If Cain is avenged sevenfold, / then Lamech seventy-sevenfold" (Gen 4:23-24). The law of Moses. however, limited retaliation: "Anyone who inflicts an injury on his neighbor shall receive the same in return. Limb for limb, eye for eye, tooth for tooth! The same injury that a man gives another shall be inflicted on him in return" (Lev 24:19-20).

Jesus brought the teachings of the Old Testament to completion. He taught, "You have heard that it was said, 'An eye for an eye and a tooth for a tooth.' But I say to you, offer no resistance to one who is evil. When someone strikes you on [your] right cheek, turn the other one to him as well" (Mt 5:38-39). Jesus taught, "You have heard that it was said, 'You shall love your neighbor and hate your enemy.' But I say to you, love your enemies, and pray for those who persecute you, that you may be children of your heavenly Father" (Mt 5:43-45).

Jesus Christ came as the fullness of God's revelation to the human race. God had spoken in partial and varied ways in the past; now he spoke his complete Word to humanity in Jesus. God's people had only glimpses of his plan; in Jesus Christ, the Word become flesh, the mystery of God's plan was revealed. Paul wrote, "When you read this you can understand my insight into the mystery of Christ, which was not made known to human beings in other generations as it has now been revealed to his holy apostles and prophets by the Spirit" (Eph 3:4-5).

Because of the revelation of God that we have in Jesus Christ, we can read the Old Testament with a fuller understanding. We can read many passages in it as a foreshadowing of Jesus, even when these passages only offer a partial glimpse of God's plan in sending us his Son. Early Christians read and understood the

Old Testament in this way, and found enrichment for their spiritual lives.

Many of the Old Testament passages that foreshadow Jesus were not written with him explicitly in mind. Psalm 2 was most likely composed to celebrate the coronation of a king of Israel; Psalm 110 probably referred to the king ruling Israel at the time it was written. But if we read these psalms with Jesus in mind, we find them fulfilled in Jesus — filled with fuller meaning. Both are quoted by New Testament writers as prophetic references to Jesus. In Acts, Paul applies the words of Psalm 2 to Jesus: "You are my son; this day I have begotten you" (Acts 13:33; Ps 2:7). The opening words of Psalm 110 — "The LORD says to you, my lord, / 'Take your throne at my right hand, / while I make your enemies your footstool'" (Ps 110:1) — are applied to Jesus several times in the New Testament, including by Jesus himself (Mk 12:35-37). Peter quotes them to proclaim the Lordship of Jesus in his Pentecost sermon (Acts 2:34-35), and the letter to the Hebrews uses them to teach that Jesus is superior to angels (Hebrews 1:13).

We can profitably read and understand the Old Testament in the light of the New.

Likewise, many passages from the prophets can be understood as dim foreshadowing of Jesus made clear by the light of his coming. We are able to understand the words of the prophets in a fuller sense than the first listeners were able to because we have received God's full revelation in Jesus Christ.

Our safest guide in applying Old Testament passages to Jesus is the New Testament. We should pay attention to the way the New Testament uses the passage from the Old Testament that it applies to Jesus. If the edition of the Bible that we are reading provides the Old Testament reference for such quotes, we can turn to the original Old Testament passages and read them with fuller understanding.

We should be cautious in giving any passage from Scripture a meaning beyond that intended by the author. Any fuller interpretation should always grow out of the meaning that the author conveyed to his first readers and be consistent with the rest of God's revelation. But we can profitably read and understand the Old Testament in the light of the New; we can understand the partial and varied ways God revealed himself in the past in the light of the revelation made to us in Jesus Christ.

The Word of Life

Jesus proclaimed that "this is the will of my Father, that everyone who sees the Son and believes in him may have eternal life, and I shall raise him [on] the last day" (Jn 6:40). To claim to be able to raise the dead of the earth to life at the end of time is a bold claim indeed. But Jesus did not back away from his claim. He instead emphasized that the words he spoke were words that gave life to those who embraced them: "It is the spirit that gives life, while the flesh is of no avail. The words I have spoken to you are spirit and life" (Jn 6:63). Peter recognized the power and promise of Jesus' words and confessed, "You have the words of eternal life" (Jn 6:68).

The disciples were not invited only to learn truths about God from Jesus but invited to know God himself. They were asked by Jesus to become what Luke calls "ministers of the word" (Lk 1:2), servants of Jesus and his message. Their mission was to make the Word of God present to women and men. The book that resulted from their ministry, the New Testament, is less concerned to teach us facts about God than to tell us how to enter into a relationship with him.

> The true meaning of the Scriptures ... is inseparable from their goal, which is to put believers into a personal relationship with God.
>
> — John Paul II, address of April 23, 1993,
> on the interpretation of the Bible in the Church

We can know a great many facts about someone but not really know him or her if we have never met that person. We can know their age, height, weight, occupation; but no matter how many of these facts are added up, we would still not know them if we had never seen them face-to-face. In the Hebrew mentality, to know was to experience; to know someone was to be intimately united with him or her. Thus Genesis states that "The man had relations with his wife Eve" — literally, "knew" his wife, Eve — "and she conceived and bore Cain" (Gen 4:1). Paul speaks of Jesus as one "who did not know sin" (2 Cor 5:21). Jesus obviously knew what sin was; Paul's meaning is that Jesus did not sin.

Eternal life comes from hearing the word of God and through it knowing God, entering into a relationship with him.

When Jesus speaks of the Son knowing the Father and the Father knowing the Son (Mt 11:27), he is talking of the intimate union of the Father and the Son. And when Jesus in his prayer to the Father says that "this is eternal life, that they should know you, the only true God, and the one whom you sent, Jesus Christ" (Jn 17:3), he is speaking of knowing the Father in the sense of being united with him. Eternal life comes from hearing the word of God and through it *knowing* God, entering into a relationship with him. The words of Jesus are words of life because they enable us to know the Father and enter into a relationship with God as his children.

The basic revelation that comes through Scripture is the revelation of God himself. The Bible is unlike any other book because through the inspiration of the Holy Spirit, inspiring its writing and inspiring our reading, we can hear words of eternal life, we can come to know God, we can enter into a relationship with God.

Our reading of the Scripture should be an encounter with the God who reveals himself through the words of Scripture. We must be attentive to what Jesus revealed about himself, what he told us about his Father, and what he promised to give us through the Holy Spirit. In order to read Scripture as the word of God, we must be filled with a desire to grow in union with God — Father, Son, and Holy Spirit.

In His goodness and wisdom God chose to reveal Himself and to make known to us the hidden purpose of His will (see Ephesians 1:9) by which through Christ, the Word made flesh, man might in the Holy Spirit have access to the Father and come to share in the divine nature (see Ephesians 2:18; 2 Pet 1:4). Through this revelation, therefore, the invisible God (see Col 1;15, 1 Tim 1:17) out of the abundance of His love speaks to men as friends (see Ex 33:11; Jn 15:14-15) and lives among them (see Baruch 3:38), so that He may invite and take them into fellowship with Himself.... By this revelation then, the deepest truth about God and the salvation of man shines out for our sake in Christ, who is both the mediator and the fullness of all revelation.

— *DIVINE REVELATION*, NO. 2

"Abba"

Jesus in the Gospels refers to God as his Father and prays to him as Father. He does so about 170 times in the Gospels, most frequently in the Gospel of John. This contrasts with previous Jewish practice: there are only about twenty references in all of the Old Testament to God as Father, and the term is used almost exclusively for God as the Father of the whole Israelite people. For example, Psalm 103 proclaims, "As a father has compassion on his children, / so the LORD has compassion on the faithful" (Psalm 103:13). Jesus, however, speaks of God as "my Father."

More significantly, the Aramaic word Jesus used to refer to his Father was *abba,* an informal and affectionate word that might best be translated as "dad." Grown children as well as children just learning to speak would call their father *abba,* and that is how Jesus spoke to God as his Father. In Gethsemane, Jesus prayed, "Abba, Father, all things are possible to you. Take this cup away from me, but not what I will but what you will" (Mk 14:36).

To refer to God as "my Father" would probably have been considered presumptuous by devout Jews at the time of Jesus, and addressing God as *Abba* was startling. Yet Jesus did so, claiming such a familiar relationship with God that the informal and intimate term *Abba* was appropriate. Jesus claimed that God was his Father and that the relationship between them was so close and loving that he could speak to God as a child to father.

This special relationship with God lay at the heart of Jesus' life and mission. He is the Son of God. All that he did, all that he taught, all that he accomplished was on the basis of him being the Son of God.

> "All things have been handed over to me by my Father. No one knows who the Son is except the Father, and who the Father is except the Son and anyone to whom the Son wishes to reveal him."
>
> — Lk 10:22

Jesus revealed God to be our Father. The parable of the Prodigal Son (Lk 15:11-32) is really the parable of the loving father, searching the horizon for the return of his lost son, forgiving him without hesitation, welcoming him back with a party. Our Father in heaven is a Father whose love goes far beyond the love that human parents have for their children:

> "If you then, who are wicked, know how to give good gifts to your children, how much more will your heavenly Father give good things to those who ask him?"
>
> — Mt 7:11

He is a Father who knows our every need (Mt 6:32) and who has prepared an eternal home for us: "Do not be afraid any longer, little flock, for your Father is pleased to give you the kingdom" (Lk 12:32).

Jesus spent much time in prayer talking with his Father, sometimes even all night (Lk 6:12). Being with the Father in prayer was an expression of his Sonship.

> He was praying in a certain place, and when he had finished, one of his disciples said to him, "Lord, teach us to pray just as John taught his disciples." He said to them, "When you pray, say:
> Father, hallowed be your name."
>
> — Lk 11:1-2

Jesus authorized his followers to address his Father as he did. He lets us be so bold as to say to God, "Our Father." He told Mary Magdalene, "Go to my brothers and tell them, 'I am going to my Father and your Father, to my God and your God'" (Jn 20:17). The Son of God makes us his brothers and sisters, children of his Father, sharing in his intimate and loving relationship with his Father.

Jesus revealed who God is: God is our Father. Jesus was able to bring us that revelation because God was his Father. Jesus taught us about God and enabled us to enter into a relationship with God, such that we can call upon him as "Abba, Father." Through Jesus, we can see the Father and have access to him.

The Way, the Truth, the Life, the Pattern

In John's Gospel, Jesus makes a very bold claim: "I am the way and the truth and the life. No one comes to the Father except through me" (Jn 14:6). What is the way of Jesus? What is the truth that he reveals? What is the life that he promises us? What does he ask of us?

"I am the way and the truth and the life. No one comes to the Father except through me. If you know me, then you will also know my Father. From now on you do know him and have seen him. . . . Whoever has seen me has seen the Father. How can you say, 'Show us the Father'? Do you not believe that I am in the Father and the Father is in me? The words that I speak to you I do not speak on my own. The Father who dwells in me is doing his works. Believe me that I am in the Father and the Father is in me."

— Jn 14:6-7, 9-11

The way: "Follow me" (Mt 9:9). Jesus' invitation to his disciples was quite simple: "Follow me." For women and men to come to know the Father and to become his daughters and sons, they had to be with and follow Jesus. The way to the Father is the way of Jesus. The call that Jesus addresses to us today is the same call: *Follow me.*

To follow Jesus means to make him the focus of our lives, our top priority. His way of life must become our way of life, for the way to the Father is the way of Jesus.

"There is no salvation through anyone else, nor is there any other name under heaven given to the human race by which we are to be saved."

— Acts 4:12

Hence the importance of our responding to his call, "Follow me," when we hear it. Jesus is the Word of God to us, the access to the Father provided for us. He is the Way, "for through him we both have access in one Spirit to the Father" (Eph 2:18).

The truth: "Whoever has seen me has seen the Father" (Jn 14:9) When people saw Jesus, what did they see? Save for his moment of transfiguration on the mountain, he looked like a normal human being. His neighbors in Nazareth apparently saw nothing extraordinary in his appearance (see Mt 13:54-58). Even after his resurrection from the dead, Jesus did not appear to people in a dazzling light: Mary Magdalene mistook him for a gardener (Jn 20:15).

The clue to seeing the Father in Jesus is provided by Jesus himself:

> "Believe me that I am in the Father and the Father is in me,
> or else, believe because of the works themselves."
>
> — Jn 14:11

The works of Jesus give us a glimpse of his Father's love in action. When Jesus wanted to summarize what he was doing, he said, "... the blind regain their sight, the lame walk, lepers are cleansed, the deaf hear, the dead are raised, and the poor have the good news proclaimed to them" (Mt 11:5). The works that Jesus did were an assault on the reign of evil in the world. Just as we are concerned when our children are sick or hungry, so our heavenly Father is concerned for us in our suffering. By his works of love, Jesus revealed his Father's love for us. Jesus as the Son is able to reveal his Father (Lk 10:22) and he brings us the truth about God: God is our loving Father.

The works of Jesus give us a glimpse of his Father's love in action.

The life: "I am the resurrection and the life" (Jn 11:25). Lazarus was a good friend of Jesus. After Lazarus died, his sister Martha told Jesus "Lord, if you had been here, my brother would not have died" (Jn 11:21). She had faith that Jesus could have preserved Lazarus from death, no matter how gravely ill he might have been. And she had the even greater faith that God would restore Lazarus to life if Jesus asked him to: "Even now I know that whatever you ask of God, God will give you" (Jn 11:22). But Jesus invited her to a yet far greater act of faith:

> Jesus told her, "I am the resurrection and the life; who-
> ever believes in me, even if he dies, will live, and everyone

who lives and believes in me will never die. Do you believe this?"

— JN 11:25-26

Our ultimate act of faith in Jesus is that in and through him we have eternal life.

In John's Gospel, Jesus makes staggering claims about himself:

"I am the living bread that came down from heaven; whoever eats this bread will live forever; and the bread that I will give is my flesh for the life of the world."

— JN 6:51

Those who heard his words were taken aback by them, saying, "How can this man give us [his] flesh to eat?" (Jn 6:52). Jesus responded by solemnly assuring them:

"Amen, amen, I say to you, unless you eat the flesh of the Son of Man and drink his blood, you do not have life within you. Whoever eats my flesh and drinks my blood has eternal life, and I will raise him on the last day."

— JN 6:53-54

Jesus is the life — eternal life. Jesus gives himself to us in the Eucharist to nourish us and to unite us with him so that we may have eternal life. God reveals himself through Jesus so that, as the Second Vatican Council proclaimed, he may take us into fellowship with himself *(Divine Revelation,* no. 2), the unending fellowship of eternal life.

The pattern: "I have given you a model to follow" (Jn 13:15). Along with Jesus being the way, the truth, and the life, Jesus is also the pattern, the model for how we are to behave. Jesus' works were not only signs of God's love; they were works to be performed by Jesus' followers in imitation of him.

"Amen, amen, I say to you, whoever believes in me will do the works that I do, and will do greater ones than these, because I am going to the Father."

— JN 14:12

The works that we are to do in imitation of Jesus are his works of love.

"I give you a new commandment: love one another. As I have loved you, so you also should love one another. This is how all will know that you are my disciples, if you have love for one another."

— JN 13:34-35

Jesus' "new commandment" is indeed new. The Old Testament law read, "You shall love your neighbor as yourself" (Lev 19:18). Jesus reaffirmed this law during his public ministry (Mt 19:19; 22:39; Mk 12:31; Lk 10:27). But during the intimacy of the Last Supper, Jesus revealed a new law for his disciples to follow: not merely love of others according to the standard by which we love ourselves, but love of others according to the standard set by Jesus.

Jesus demonstrated the meaning of the new command by washing his disciples' feet during the Last Supper. This was a lowly service usually performed by a household slave, and Peter rebelled at the idea of Jesus washing his feet (Jn 13:8). But Jesus nevertheless washed their feet and then told them, "I have given you a model to follow, so that as I have done for you, you should also do" (Jn 13:15). His love was a love of humble service, a love that went far beyond merely extending self-love to others. It was a radically self-sacrificing love.

> During the intimacy of the Last Supper, Jesus revealed a new law for his disciples to follow: not merely love of others according to the standard by which we love ourselves, but love of others according to the standard set by Jesus.

Jesus loved his disciples to the point of death:

"This is my commandment: love one another as I love you. No one has greater love than this, to lay down one's life for one's friends."

— JN 15:12-13

Jesus could not have made the meaning of his new commandment any clearer than by presenting it to his disciples on the eve of his death. "As I have loved you, so you also should love one another" (Jn 13:34).

In Jesus we see the Father; in the love that Jesus has for us, we see the love that our Father has for us. In following Jesus we have our way to the Father. Although Jesus does not physically walk in our midst today, he is still with us (Mt 18:20; 28:20). As the way, the truth, and the life, Jesus is the revelation of God. He gives us not merely knowledge about God, but knowledge of God; not merely a message from a distant God, but a path to our Father. He gives us a pattern to follow so that we may inherit eternal life. And he gives us all this through his Holy Spirit.

The Spirit of God

In all four Gospels, John the Baptist proclaims Jesus to be the one who will enable men and women to be immersed in the Holy Spirit: "I have baptized you with water; he will baptize you with the holy Spirit" (Mk 1:8; see also Mt 3:11; Lk 3:16; Jn 1:33). Jesus promised that he would send the Spirit as living waters for the thirsty (Jn 7:37-39), as one who would lead us into the truth (Jn 14:26; 16:13), as the power of God present in our lives (Lk 24:49; Acts 1:4-5, 8). The life that Jesus brings is the life of the Spirit.

On Pentecost, the Holy Spirit descended and the Church sprang to life. Where before the disciples had been fearful and uncertain (Jn 20:19), with the power of the Spirit they were bold in proclaiming the word of God (Acts 4:29-31).

The presence of the Spirit in our lives is more than a matter of boldness. The Spirit makes us adopted children of God:

> For those who are led by the Spirit of God are children of God. For you did not receive a spirit of slavery to fall back into fear, but you received a spirit of adoption, through which we cry, "Abba, Father!" The Spirit itself bears witness with our spirit that we are children of God.
>
> — Rom 8:14-16

Jesus taught us about our heavenly Father; the Holy Spirit present in us enables us to address God as Abba, just as Jesus himself did. "As proof that you are children, God sent the spirit of his Son into our hearts, crying out, 'Abba, Father!'" (Gal 4:6). The Holy Spirit that filled and guided Jesus (Lk 4:1, 14, 18-21) lives in us to guide and empower us to follow in the footsteps of Jesus.

The Holy Spirit that filled and guided Jesus (Lk 4:1, 14, 18-21) lives in us to guide and empower us to follow in the footsteps of Jesus.

The hallmarks of the presence of the Spirit in our lives — "love, joy, peace, patience, kindness, generosity, faithfulness, gentleness, self-control" (Gal 5:22-23) — were characteristics of the life of Jesus. We have the power to sacrifice ourselves in love, just as Jesus sacrificed himself in love, through the Holy Spirit. We receive true joy from the Holy Spirit, as Jesus did: "At that very moment he rejoiced [in] the holy Spirit" (Lk 10:21). The peace of Jesus that he promised to us is the peace that is a fruit of the Spirit (Gal 5:22): "Peace I leave with you; my peace I give to you" (Jn 14:27).

After discussing the gifts of the Holy Spirit (1 Cor 12:1-31), Paul wrote that even more excellent is love (1 Cor 13:32). Love is Jesus' new command: to love as he loved. Such a love to the point of self-sacrificing death is beyond our own capability. We need the power of the Spirit to love as Jesus loved. God so loved the world that he sent his Son to us (Jn 3:16). God so loves the world now that he gives us the power to love with his love through the Spirit living in us.

There are different ways to express the mystery of what it means to be a Christian. We can say that to be a Christian is to be adopted as sons and daughters of God. We can say that to be a Christian is to be in Christ and a member of the body of Christ. We can say that to be a Christian is to be filled with the Holy Spirit. All of these statements speak of the same mystery and express aspects of it in terms of our relationship with the Father, or with Jesus Christ, or with the Holy Spirit. But although there are three persons in God, there is one God and one mystery of him drawing us to himself.

> What ultimately makes the words of Scripture unlike any other words is the reality behind them: the plan of the Father to adopt us as his children through Jesus, giving us the life of the Holy Spirit.

We read Scripture within this context of God giving us life and drawing us to himself. What ultimately makes the words of Scripture unlike any other words is the reality behind them: the plan of the Father to adopt us as his children through Jesus, giving us the life of the Holy Spirit. Hence, the role of the Holy Spirit in our reading is more than a matter of giving understanding to our minds and touching our hearts. His role is most basically to give us life — God's life. Our reading of Scripture is an occasion for our growing in that life.

To "inspire" is, literally, to "breathe in." The Holy Spirit inspires our reading in order that he may literally inspire life into us, that he may be the breath of God breathed into us. One of the authors of Genesis conceived of the creation of the first human in this way:

> The LORD God formed man out of the clay of the ground and blew into his nostrils the breath of life, and so man became a living being.
>
> — GEN 2:7

John's Gospel tells us that after Jesus' resurrection he sent his disciples out to carry on his mission, "and when he had said this, he breathed on them and said to them, 'Receive the holy Spirit'" (Jn 20:22). The Word of God to us is a breath of life.

Jesus came so that we might receive the Holy Spirit and be an inspired people, a Spirit-filled people. The plan of Jesus was to create a Church in which his Spirit would live and through which people would come to know God's love for them. It is God who speaks to us through the words of Scripture; it is, above all, the Church who hears this word of life.

Resources

The opening chapter of the Second Vatican Council's *Dogmatic Constitution on Divine Revelation* is on "Divine Revelation Itself," and is worth careful reading and reflection.

Study Guide

1. How much of the Old Testament have I read in the course of my life? What portions of it have the most appeal and meaning for me? What portions do I find difficult to understand? What are the most important lessons I have learned from the Old Testament?

2. Jesus brought to completion the teaching of the Old Testament. When some Old Testament teaching puzzles me, do I try to recall or search out what Jesus had to say on the topic? Do I try to interpret what I read in the Old Testament in light of Jesus?

3. The basic revelation that comes through Scripture is the revelation of God himself. How has God made himself known to me? What role is reading Scripture playing in my coming to know God better?

4. What is God like for me? What is my image of God? What is the significance of Jesus' calling God his Father? What is the significance of Jesus' authorizing us to pray to God as our Father?

5. What does it mean for me to follow Jesus as his disciple? What does he require of me? Where is he leading me?

6. Which of Jesus' many miracles and acts of mercy most appeal to me? Why? What do they reveal about Jesus? What do they reveal about the one who sent him?

7. Jesus said, "Whoever has seen me has seen the Father" (Jn 14:9). What does God look like seen in the mirror of Jesus? How would I characterize God, if God is revealed in Jesus?

8. Jesus said, "As I have loved you, so you also should love one another" (Jn 13:34). How has Jesus loved me? How does Jesus ask me to love?

9. What do I live for? What are my ultimate hopes? How firm is my faith that Jesus Christ offers me resurrection to eternal life? How often do I think about the eternal life Jesus offers me? How thoroughly does my hope of eternal life shape my life here and now?

10. What is my image of the Holy Spirit? What role does he play in my spiritual life? What role should he play in my reading of Scripture? Have I ever been conscious of receiving his help as I read the Bible?

SEVEN

It Is the Church Who Listens

They devoted themselves to the teaching of the apostles and to the communal life, to the breaking of the bread and to the prayers. Awe came upon everyone, and many wonders and signs were done through the apostles. All who believed were together and had all things in common; they would sell their property and possessions and divide them among all according to each one's need. Every day they devoted themselves to meeting together in the temple area and to breaking bread in their homes. They ate their meals with exultation and sincerity of heart, praising God and enjoying favor with all the people. And every day the Lord added to their number those who were being saved.

— Acts 2:42-47

Pentecost was a turning point. After the risen Jesus ascended into heaven, his followers huddled together in the upper room, waiting for the coming of the Holy Spirit who had been promised (Lk 24:49; Acts 1:4-5, 8). They were relatively few in number, only about one hundred and twenty (Acts 1:15).

If their past performance was any indication, not too much could be expected from them. The men had deserted Jesus when he was arrested (Mk 14:50). Even after his resurrection, they had been fearful and slow to believe (Mt 28:17; Mk 16:8; Lk 24:11, 25, 37; Jn 20:19, 25).

Pentecost transformed this unpromising group into a dynamic Church. The Holy Spirit gave them the power to boldly proclaim the message of Jesus (Acts 4:29-31). The inspiration of the Holy Spirit gave them the insight to understand how the Old Testament Scriptures were fulfilled in Jesus (Acts 2:16-36).

In Luke's presentation of the events in Acts, the early Church seems to spring forth full-grown on Pentecost. In the aftermath of the coming of the Holy Spirit, the followers of Christ join together for prayers and for the basic pattern of their lives. People who must have been strangers before, people of different languages even (Acts 2:8-11), begin sharing their possessions with one another, finding the focus of their lives in what they have in common in Jesus Christ.

After Pentecost, the context of the New Testament is the early Church. There are great personalities who capture our attention, particularly Paul. But Luke focuses on Paul in the last half of Acts to show how the Church spread "to the ends of the earth" (Acts 1:8). Paul did not volunteer for his first missionary journey; the Church in Antioch, acting under the inspiration of the Holy Spirit, selected him and sent him out (Acts 13:1-3).

Today, we may be tempted to think that membership in the Church is something separate from belief in Jesus Christ. Or we may conceive of membership in the Church as a part-time concern, something that is not at the center of our lives. Either attitude would have been unthinkable in the early Church.

Peter's sermon on Pentecost day was a proclamation that Jesus, raised from the dead, was Lord and Messiah (Acts 2:32, 36). When people's hearts were touched and they asked him, "What are we to do?" Peter replied, "Repent and be baptized, every one of you, in the name of Jesus Christ for the forgiveness of your sins; and you will receive the gift of the holy Spirit" (Acts 2:37-38). Peter did not say, "You must join the Church." Peter simply said *repent, be baptized, receive the Holy Spirit.* But the result of women and men repenting, being baptized, and receiving the

Holy Spirit was the creation of the Church: "about three thousand persons were added that day" (Acts 2:41). The result of Peter's proclamation was the creation of a fellowship, centered on prayer and nourished by the teaching of the apostles. There is no grounds in Acts for divorcing belief in Jesus Christ from membership in his Church.

Nor was membership in the early Church a limited commitment, a duty to be discharged by worshipping together once a week. Membership in the early Church was a matter of one's whole life being joined with other Christians. The things that people held dearest — possessions and time — were put in common. While not every early Church community followed the same pattern of common ownership as the Jerusalem community, it is clear that joining the early Church meant a rather complete reorganization of one's life.

> While not every early Church community followed the same pattern of common ownership as the Jerusalem community, it is clear that joining the early Church meant a rather complete reorganization of one's life.

When we compare the state of things before and after Pentecost day, it is clear that the Holy Spirit played an indispensable role. Without the power and guidance of the Holy Spirit, the disciples may have died of old age in the upper room. With the Holy Spirit, thousands completely reorganized their lives around fellowship in Jesus Christ.

In order to more fully understand this fellowship, we need to reflect on how Jesus carried out his mission during his public ministry. And this, in turn, will provide us with the key to understanding the place of Scripture in the Church.

The Plan of Jesus

If we were to read the Gospels as if for the first time, we might be struck by how unlikely an approach Jesus took in his mission. Jesus did none of the things that we would do if we set out to change the course of history.

Rome was the political center of the Western world at the time of Jesus; if we had wanted to influence the world, we would have chosen Rome for our starting point. God did not. Instead, he chose to send his Son as a Galilean Jew, a member of an inconsequential people without political power. If we were to forego political means for influencing history, we might choose the influence of ideas. But Galilee was far from the intellectual center of the world. In the realm of philosophy, no ancient civilization matched Greece in the time of Socrates, Plato, and Aristotle. Yet Jesus was not born a Greek, so that he could be a disciple of Aristotle.

If we were to read the Gospels as if for the first time, we might be struck by how unlikely an approach Jesus took in his mission. Jesus did none of the things that we would do if we set out to change the course of history.

If we could not influence the political or intellectual trends of our time, we would at least try to attract a large following for ourselves. Here again, the focus of Jesus was different. While Jesus did preach to the multitudes, he spent most of his time with a small number of disciples. Most of his effort went into preparing this band of followers to carry on his mission. His emphasis was not on numbers: he rejected an attempt by a crowd to make him king (Jn 6:15), and he never watered down his hard sayings to keep the allegiance of half-hearted followers (Jn 6:60-66).

The strategy that Jesus followed was to select a small number of rather ordinary people, ask them to wholeheartedly dedicate their lives to him, and train them to carry out his mission. His basic training program was to invite them to live with him. When he invited someone to follow him, his words meant literally that: to follow him as he walked the countryside of Galilee.

Jesus' choice of followers is noteworthy. He did not single out religious leaders or scholars. His band of followers was made up of pretty ordinary people. As we see them described in the Gospels, none of them strike us as very likely candidates for undertaking great responsibilities. But it was this group of people that received most of Jesus' time and attention. He taught them, he counseled them, he sent them out on a practice mission. Most basically, he let them live with him and he loved them. He taught them the meaning of love by his love for them (Jn 13:1, 34); he taught them to take on his mission by his example in carrying it out himself. He focused on preparing a small group of ordinary people who could be the seed, the nucleus of his Church.

We should note that Jesus did not write a book. If written words were to be the all-important focus in his Church, we would have expected him to leave us something in writing. Most world leaders put down their vision in books and articles, but Jesus left no written manifesto behind. Since it would have been easy for him to have done so, we must interpret this as a deliberate choice on his part. Nor did Jesus choose followers who would make particularly good writers. Scribes, who were trained writers, aren't noted as being among his followers. Had Jesus placed great emphasis on getting his teachings set down in writing, he could have chosen someone to transcribe them, as Jeremiah had Baruch write down his prophecies (Jer 36:4). There is no evidence, however, that Jesus did so.

> Just as the focus of Jesus was not on political power, or intellectual trends, or large numbers of followers, it was not on the written word. Instead, his focus was on his word embodied in the lives of his followers, on his word living on in and through them.

Just as the focus of Jesus was not on political power, or intellectual trends, or large numbers of followers, it was not on the written word. Instead, his focus was on his word embodied in the lives of his followers, on his word living on in and through them. Under the inspiration of the Holy Spirit, they would live the new command of love and be so united among themselves that the world, seeing them, would believe that Jesus Christ was truly the Son of God, and through that belief find life (Jn 17:20-21; 20:31). The people of God were to be the word of God.

It is in this context that we can understand the birth of the Church described in Acts. The Holy Spirit did not create something from nothing: he completed the work that Jesus had begun. Once the apostles had received the outpouring of the Holy Spirit, the Church could come into its full life because of Jesus' years of teaching and preparation. The Church in turn is the context in which the New Testament Scriptures came to be written.

The Handing-On

Paul summarized the core message he preached:

> Now I am reminding you, brothers, of the gospel I preached to you, which you indeed received and in which you also stand... For I handed on to you as of first importance what I also received: that Christ died for our sins in accordance with the scriptures; that he was buried; that he was raised on the third day in accordance with the scriptures; that he appeared to Kephas, then to the Twelve.
>
> — 1 COR 15:1, 3-5

Paul wrote that he "handed on" to others the message that he himself had received. The Greek word that Paul used for "handed on" is the word that gives us, through its Latin equivalent, the word "tradition." Paul told the Corinthians that their faith was based on the message that he himself had received and that he had faithfully handed on to them. And that is the root meaning of "tradition": the handing-on of the Gospel message.

For several decades, the handing-on was done by word-of-mouth preaching.

Jesus brought us the revelation of saving truth from God and commissioned his followers to hand it on to others.

> "Go, therefore, and make disciples of all nations, baptizing them in the name of the Father, and of the Son, and of the holy Spirit, teaching them to observe all that I have

commanded you. And behold, I am with you always, until the end of the age."

— MT 28:19-20

From the preaching of the apostles, under the power and guidance of the Holy Spirit, the Church began.

For several decades, the handing-on was done by word-of-mouth preaching. The first book of the New Testament to be written was Paul's first letter to the Church in Thessalonica, written about twenty years after the resurrection and ascension of Jesus. None of the Gospels in the form we have them can be securely dated prior to around A.D. 70, and the Gospel of John was not completed until around the end of the first century. So, to hear the saving truth about Jesus Christ meant literally to *hear* it. To accept the Gospel was to accept the living tradition that was being handed on in the Church.

Paul's letters bristle with references to his verbal handing-on of the Gospel:

> I praise you because you remember me in everything and hold fast to the traditions, just as I handed them on to you.
>
> — 1 COR 11:2

> We instruct you, brothers, in the name of [our] Lord Jesus Christ, to shun any brother who conducts himself in a disorderly way and not according to the tradition they received from us.
>
> — 2 THESS 3:6

Timothy is instructed to train others to hand on the message:

> And what you heard from me through many witnesses entrust to faithful people who will have the ability to teach others as well.
>
> — 2 TIM 2:2

The books of the New Testament were written to meet the needs of the growing Church. As the number of churches that Paul founded grew, he could not meet their needs by his personal presence. Hence he wrote them letters, most often to resolve specific problems, offer encouragement in the face of their difficulties, and answer questions that had arisen. Paul considered his letters to carry his authority and to be a part of handing on the Gospel tradition:

> The books of the New Testament were written to meet the needs of the growing Church.

> Therefore, brothers, stand firm and hold fast to the traditions that you were taught, either by an oral statement or by a letter of ours.
>
> — 2 Thess 2:15

Some letters were also meant to be passed from one church community to the next (Col 4:16).

> The Church has always venerated the divine Scriptures just as she venerates the body of the Lord, since, especially in the sacred liturgy, she unceasingly receives and offers to the faithful the bread of life from the table both of God's word and of Christ's body. She has always maintained them, and continues to do so, together with sacred tradition, as the supreme rule of faith, since, as inspired by God and committed once and for all to writing, they impart the word of God Himself without change, and make the voice of the Holy Spirit resound in the words of the prophets and Apostles. Therefore, like the Christian religion itself, all the preaching of the Church must be nourished and regulated by Sacred Scripture. For in the sacred books, the Father who is in heaven meets His children with great love and speaks with them.
>
> — *Divine Revelation*, no. 21

The Gospels were written to preserve this living tradition. Luke, who had not known Jesus during his life on earth, set out to write down the tradition that was handed on: remembrances of the words of Jesus that were passed on by word of mouth, written fragments containing these sayings, and most likely a copy of Mark's Gospel. Luke began his Gospel by stating this purpose in writing it, addressing himself to a certain Theophilus:

> Since many have undertaken to compile a narrative of the events that have been fulfilled among us, just as those who were eyewitnesses from the beginning and ministers of the word have handed them down to us, I too have decided, after investigating everything accurately anew, to write it down in an orderly sequence for you.
>
> — LK 1:1-3

Luke wished to faithfully compile the oral and written tradition into a careful account. He wished to be faithful to the traditions as they had been "handed . . down to us."

Under the guidance of the Holy Spirit, the New Testament writers did more than simply try to recount Jesus' every word and deed. From the very outset, the Church had to face new questions and new situations. Even in the years immediately following the resurrection of Jesus, the Gospel was not a dead letter, a rigid remembrance of the word that Jesus taught, but a living handing-on, guided by the Holy Spirit, confronting new questions and situations.

Even in the years immediately following the resurrection of Jesus, the Gospel was not a dead letter, a rigid remembrance of the word that Jesus taught, but a living handing-on, guided by the Holy Spirit, confronting new questions and situations.

The first major crisis affecting the Church was the question of how Gentiles could be admitted to the Church. The ministry of Jesus was largely limited to Jews. On Pentecost, Jews from many countries came into the Church. While they accepted

Jesus as the Messiah, they were still Jews and continued to worship in the Temple: "Every day they devoted themselves to meeting together in the temple area" (Acts 2:46). The earliest Church was a segment of Judaism. If non-Jews came to faith in Jesus as the Christ, how should they be received? Should they be required to convert to Judaism and obey the entire Law of Moses? Nothing in Jesus' explicit teaching seemed to resolve the question.

> The common prayer life of the early Church — its liturgy — sometimes influenced the way the good news of Jesus Christ was expressed.

How this question was settled is one of the dramas underlying the book of Acts and some of Paul's letters. A solution was found under the guidance of the Holy Spirit:

> The apostles and the presbyters, your brothers, to the brothers in Antioch, Syria, and Cilicia of Gentile origin:...
> It is the decision of the holy Spirit and of us not to place on you any burden beyond these necessities.
>
> — ACTS 15:23, 28

The needs of the early Church also influenced their remembrance of what Jesus did and taught and which elements were handed on in their teaching. The Gospel of John notes that "Jesus did many other signs in the presence of [his] disciples that are not written in this book" (Jn 20:30). The Holy Spirit guided the evangelists in selecting material for their renditions of the Gospel. They shaped their Gospels in accordance with their purposes in writing. John's Gospel was "written that you may [come to] believe that Jesus is the Messiah, the Son of God, and that through this belief you may have life in his name" (Jn 20:31).

The common prayer life of the early Church — its liturgy — sometimes influenced the way the good news of Jesus Christ was expressed. Paul wrote to the Christians of Corinth:

> I received from the Lord what I also handed on to you, that the Lord Jesus, on the night he was handed over, took bread, and, after he had given thanks, broke it and said, "This is my body that is for you. Do this in remembrance of me." In the same way also the cup, after supper, saying, "This cup is the new covenant in my blood. Do this, as often as you drink it, in remembrance of me."
>
> — 1 COR 11:23-25

The Lord's Supper was celebrated for several decades before Paul wrote his letters to Corinth, and for even longer before the Gospel accounts of the Last Supper were written. The words of Jesus were remembered in "the breaking of the bread" (Acts 2:42). Through their repetition in the liturgy, they came to be expressed in set ways. When Paul wrote to Corinth about the Last Supper, the words he used were words already in use in the liturgy of the early Church.

Note what Paul said: "I received from the Lord what I also handed on to you" (1 Cor 11:23). Paul probably did not receive a direct revelation from Jesus telling him what happened at the Last Supper. Rather, Paul identifies what was commemorated in the liturgy with what he received from Jesus. The sense of his words is, "This is what was handed on to me by the living tradition of the Church, and this is what I in turn handed on to you."

In summary, the needs of the early Church influenced which incidents and teachings from the life of Jesus were remembered as well as the manner in which those incidents were expressed. The Gospel message was handed on by word of mouth before it was set down in written form. It was thus very important that this handing-on be guided by the Holy Spirit.

The Spirit's Guidance

We cannot limit the inspiration of Scripture to the final setting down of words in writing; the guidance of the Holy Spirit in shaping the oral tradition was also essential. The Holy Spirit inspired and guided the Church and its leaders in their decisions concerning the admission of Gentiles to baptism, the development of its forms of worship, and other important issues. The Gospel was a living word, incarnated in the life of the Church. Its final writing was as much an expression of the life of the Church as it was a writing down of something that had previously been passed on by word of mouth. Jesus' promise of the Holy Spirit was much more than a promise that a book would be written that would be free from errors. Jesus did not come to create a holy book but a holy people.

The gifts of the Spirit must be seen as an important aspect of the way the Holy Spirit guided the handing-on of the Gospel message in the early Church. He inspired preachers and teachers before he inspired writers.

Paul gives us various lists of the ways in which the Holy Spirit is present in the Church, inspiring and guiding. "To one is given through the Spirit the expression of wisdom; to another the expression of knowledge according to the same Spirit; to another faith by the same Spirit; to another gifts of healing by the one Spirit; to another mighty deeds; to another prophecy; to another discernment of spirits; to another varieties of tongues; to another interpretation of tongues" (1 Cor 12:8-10). Another list reads differently but has similar meaning: "He gave some as apostles, others as prophets, others as evangelists, others as pastors and teachers, to equip the holy ones for the work of ministry, for building up the body of Christ" (Eph 4:11-12).

The presence of the Holy Spirit in the Church was concretely manifested in gifts of service. These gifts only had meaning in the context of the Christian community; their purpose was to build up of the Church. Paul also insisted that some gifts were more valuable than others, and that the importance of all gifts could be judged by their value for the Church (1 Cor 14).

The gifts of the Spirit must be seen as an important aspect of the way the Holy Spirit guided the handing-on of the Gospel message in the early Church. He inspired preachers and teachers before he inspired writers. In fact, Paul does not even mention authors or writers in any of his lists of the ways in which the Spirit operates! This doesn't mean, however, that the writers of the New Testament weren't inspired. They were — including Paul himself when he listed the gifts of the Spirit. The point is that the focus of the Spirit's inspiration was the Church, and that he worked through a variety of gifts to provide for the teaching needs of the Church and the faithful handing-on of the message of Jesus.

When we reflect on Jesus' selection and commissioning of the apostles, and on the way the early Church resolved the question of Gentile converts, and on the teaching of Paul in his letters, it is clear that the early Church recognized certain people as authoritative teachers and leaders. There were apostles, both those whom Jesus chose and those who, like Paul, were later called apostles. There were "overseers" (Acts 20:28; Phil 1:1); the Greek word for "overseer" can be translated as "bishop" (1 Tim 3:2; Titus 1:7). There were also "presbyters" — a Greek word meaning elders — (Acts 11:30; 14:23; 15:2; 1 Tim 5:17; Titus 1:5; Jas 5:14; 1 Pet 5:5). These leaders, with the guidance of the Holy Spirit, resolved the questions facing the early Church and were the touchstone of authenticity for the handing-on of the Gospel.

While there was consultation and interaction between the apostles and the Jerusalem community regarding the need for creating assistants (who are often thought of as deacons), it was the Twelve who called the community together to deal with the issue, and it was the Twelve who laid hands on them, commissioning them (Acts 6:1-6). The Gentile convert question was resolved after "the apostles and the presbyters met together to see about this matter" (Acts 15:6). The letter to Titus lists desirable qualities for bishops; along with personal maturity and holiness, an elder must hold "fast to the true message as taught so that he will be able both to exhort with sound doctrine and to refute opponents" (Titus 1:9).

Paul's letters also reveal the crosscurrents of thoughts during the years following Jesus' ascension. Not everyone received or understood the Gospel in its purity; not everyone handed it on faithfully. Paul was opposed by those who demanded that Gentile converts follow the entire Mosaic Law; he also had to contend with the superstitions and pagan practices that new converts carried over into their Christianity. Paul had to warn people not to accept any gospel preached to them that was different from the tradition he had handed on, even if they should hear the new gospel from an angel (Gal 1:8).

A touchstone of authenticity for the true tradition was hence necessary. There could be no appeal to the Bible, for the New Testament had yet to be compiled. Not every prophetic utterance could be accepted without question, for false prophets also claimed to speak by the inspiration of the Spirit (1 Jn 4:1). The touchstone of authenticity was found within in the Church under the guidance of its apostles and leaders. It was through them that the Spirit guided the authentic handing-on of the Gospel message.

The discernment of the Church was necessary to sort out which early writings faithfully captured the tradition of the Church and which did not. The four Gospels we accept as inspired word were only four of many writings claiming to be Gospels. Some even claimed to have been written by apostles. A *Gospel of Thomas* begins by claiming, "These are the secret words which the living Jesus spoke and Didymus Judas Thomas wrote." Then follow one hundred fourteen sayings of Jesus, some very similar to the teaching of Jesus found in the four Gospels of the New Testament, but some quite different.

Writings also appeared in the early Church that claimed to be lost letters from Paul or claimed to narrate the acts of the apostles John, Andrew, and Thomas, just as the New Testament book of Acts treats the ministry of Peter and Paul. Even apocalyptic books appeared, purporting to be revelations given to Peter or Paul or Thomas.

The early Church faced an important challenge in sorting out the writings that were an authentic handing-on of the Gospel message from those that were not. It was not self-evident which books should be considered sacred Scripture and which should not. The claim that a letter was written by Paul, or that a gospel was written by Thomas, or that a revelation was given to Peter, was not enough to establish that these were indeed apostolic works. And on the other hand, just because a gospel was written by someone other than an apostle did not mean that it was to be rejected; Luke was not one of the twelve apostles.

Far from the New Testament dropping down from heaven to be the constitution and bylaws of the early Church, it was the early Church that constituted the New Testament. The individual books of the New Testament set down in words the authentic faith that the early Church was living, the faith that had been handed on under the guidance of the Holy Spirit. And it was the Church who decided which books could be used as a standard to judge the authenticity of preaching. Our word *canon* comes from a Semitic word which meant a reed used for measuring; a canonical book is one that can be accepted as a measure, a guide, a rule.

We have no evidence that there was ever a special revelation from God directly establishing the books to be accepted as canonical. Rather, the bishops of the Church decided which books were to be considered a part of the Bible, selecting twenty-seven books as an authentic expression of the faith of the Church.

The early Church faced an important challenge in sorting out the writings that were an authentic handing-on of the Gospel message from those that were not.

The bishops of the Church decided which books were to be considered a part of the Bible, selecting twenty-seven books as an authentic expression of the faith of the Church.

The discussion over which books were to be accepted as canonical lasted several hundred years. During this time, different collections of books were accepted in different parts of the Church. While there was general agreement about most of the books we read as part of the New Testament, there were a number of books that caused considerable discussion — for instance, the letter to the Hebrews. It was not until almost the year 400 that complete agreement prevailed throughout the Church that the twenty-seven books we read as the New Testament belonged in it, and no others.

It is the Church Who Listens

The first letter of John states that it is written "so that you too may have fellowship with us; / for our fellowship is with the Father / and with his Son, Jesus Christ" (1 Jn 1:3). Fellowship with the Father through Jesus Christ is inextricably linked with fellowship with other Christians, with being a part of the body of Christ.

God chose to save us not solely as individuals, but as a part of the body of Christ. The work of the Holy Spirit within us enables us to address God as Father and to graft us onto the body of Christ. To be made a son or daughter of God is to join the family of God.

> God, however, does not make men holy and save them merely as individuals, without bond or link between one another. Rather has it pleased Him to bring men together as one people, a people which acknowledges Him in truth and serves Him in holiness.
>
> — VATICAN II, *CONSTITUTION ON THE CHURCH*, NO. 9

Revelation began with the dialogue between God and his people in Old Testament times; revelation reached its fulfillment in Jesus Christ, the Word made flesh. The word of God was nurtured and handed on in the people of God. The word of God today still finds its home in the people of God. Scripture is part of the continuing dialogue between God and his people, the Church.

The words of Scripture have full meaning only for those joined to Christ through his Body. We don't merely read Scripture as individuals; we also participate in the Church's reading of Scripture, as one aspect of its life. This can be seen most clearly in the proclamation of Scripture during the liturgy, a proclamation that nourishes faith and Christian life.

That the Church is the place where we listen to the word of God is not universally understood or accepted. Some hold that the Bible is the primary way that God speaks to us, placing it apart from and above the Church. Others go even further, saying that the Bible is all that is needed and that what is important is our relationship with Jesus Christ; Church membership is optional.

> We need the guidance of the Church and the Holy Spirit in bringing the message of Scripture to bear on new situations and new questions.

Such views are unsupported by the Bible itself. The thrust of the Gospels is that Jesus worked to leave behind a family of followers who would carry on his mission. His focus was not on writing a book or even on selecting those who would be authors. The book of Acts focuses on the spread of the Church, not on the development of the Bible. The way to salvation was found through becoming part of the apostolic Church.

We need the guidance of the Church in order to properly understand Scripture. We need to be in contact with the understanding of the message of salvation that reaches back to the time of the apostles, and that was expressed in the written words of the Bible. We need the guidance of the Church and the Holy

Spirit in bringing the message of Scripture to bear on new situations and new questions.

The second letter of Peter states, "There is no prophecy of scripture that is a matter of personal interpretation, for no prophecy ever came through human will; but rather human beings moved by the holy Spirit spoke under the influence of God" (2 Pet 1:20-21). The argument seems to be that just as the prophecy contained in Scripture does not originate with human beings but with the Holy Spirit, so its interpretation is not left up to the individual. The way in which the word of God was uttered provides the context for our understanding it. God spoke through his people in both Old and New Testament times; our listening and understanding must take place within the context of his people today.

The Holy Spirit is as alive in the Church today as he was in the early Church. He did not guide the Church leaders in deciding the Gentile convert question and then abandon the Church, no longer guiding its leaders today. Nor does he, now that the Bible has been written, restrict his guidance to the written words of Scripture. He continues to be present in the Church, inspiring the handing-on of the message of salvation.

Acceptance of Scripture as the word of God implies acceptance of the way in which it came to be uttered in human language. Acceptance of Scripture implies acceptance of the tradition that formed Scripture and judged it to be inspired. Acceptance of Scripture implies acceptance of the teaching authority of the Church, since it is through that teaching authority that the words of Scripture were judged to be the authentic measure of our faith. We cannot accept an authoritative teaching role for the Church in the first century but deny it that same role today. To do so would be to claim that the Holy Spirit who guided the early Church no longer guides the Church in our time.

The role of the Church isn't to pass judgment on the truth or falsity of what is contained in Scripture, but to be nourished by

Scripture, to proclaim the message contained in Scripture, and to embody the realities set down there. The role of the Church is to continue the handing-on of the message of salvation begun in the time of the apostles. Scripture is a norm for the Church in doing this, as well as a tool. Like Paul, the Church does not merely hand on a message; it hands on life by reconciling us to God through Christ: "And all this is from God, who has reconciled us to himself through Christ and given us the ministry of reconciliation" (2 Cor 5:18).

But the task of authentically interpreting the word of God, whether written or handed on, has been entrusted exclusively to the living teaching office of the Church, whose authority is exercised in the name of Jesus Christ. This teaching office is not above the word of God, but serves it, teaching only what has been handed on, listening to it devoutly, guarding it scrupulously and explaining it faithfully in accord with a divine commission and with the help of the Holy Spirit, it draws from this one deposit of faith everything which it presents for belief as divinely revealed.

It is clear, therefore, that sacred tradition, Sacred Scripture and the teaching authority of the Church, in accord with God's most wise design, are so linked and joined together that one cannot stand without the others, and that all together and each in its own way under the action of the one Holy Spirit contribute effectively to the salvation of souls.

— *Divine Revelation*, no. 10

While the authoritative role of the Church's teaching ministry is essential, it is in the full life of the Church that our reading of Scripture finds its context and meaning. To reduce the Church to being merely a teacher, however infallible, is to focus on only one dimension of its mission. It is not only what the Church teaches but how the Church lives that provides the norm for our understanding of Scripture. Our understanding of Scripture is formed in a thousand imperceptible ways: by the preaching we hear, by our common life of worship, by our "fellowship of the holy Spirit" (2 Cor 13:13) with other Christians.

It may be easier to ascribe an otherworldly perfection to the Bible and place all our credence in it, rather than trust in a Church whose human imperfections and sinfulness can be so apparent. But God's plan was not to guide us by writing a perfect book; his plan was to incorporate us into a people on the road to salvation. Our scandal that the Church isn't more perfect was probably already felt in the first century; Peter never appeared to be flawless. It may be easier to put our faith in Scripture rather than in the Church, but such faith, if it chooses Scripture over against the Church, is misplaced: it makes Scripture out to be more and the Church to be less than they are in the plan of God.

It is the Church who listens to the word of God spoken through the Scriptures. God speaks his word to the Church so that the Church itself might be the messenger of God to the world, and the message of God to the world. The word that God spoke in Jesus Christ continues to resound in the world through the lives of those who have found life in him. The Word of God is now made present in the people of God, the Church.

Resources

All of the Second Vatican Council's *Decree on Divine Revelation* is worth careful reflection; chapters 1 (Divine Revelation Itself) and 6 (Sacred Scripture in the Life of the Church) address how the Word of God is addressed to, and should be read by, the Church.

The *Catechism of the Catholic Church* addresses the transmission of divine revelation in sections 74 to 100, and the canon of Scripture and Scripture in the life of the Church in sections 120 to 141.

Study Guide

1. What is my experience of belonging to the Church? Is it a once-a-week activity for me or something more? What link do I see between being a disciple of Jesus and being a member of the Church?

2. If I wanted to leave a lasting imprint on the world, how would I go about it? What means are at my disposal to leave at least a little imprint? If I were to die tonight, what imprint would I leave behind?

3. What are the implications for me of Jesus choosing rather ordinary women and men to be his first followers and to form the seed of his Church? If Jesus had come today, might he choose me to be one of his followers? What response would I make to him?

4. Jesus didn't write a book or ask anyone to transcribe his teachings, although he could have easily done so. What does this say to me about Jesus' priorities during his public ministry?

5. The first generations of Christians handed on the message of Jesus by word of mouth. Do I also try to hand on the saving message of Jesus Christ to others by what I say to them?

6. The four Gospels are edited versions of the Gospel message as it was passed on by word of mouth in the early Church. How should this influence the way in which I read and understand the Gospels?

7. How important was the role of the Holy Spirit in the early Church? How important is his role in the Church today? How important a role does the Holy Spirit play in my life? How has the Spirit gifted me to serve the Church? Am I making full use of the gifts and talents I have been given?

8. Which is truer: the Church created the Bible, or the Bible created the Church? What are the implications of this for how I read and interpret the Bible?

9. Reflect on the obvious but often overlooked fact that the Bible we read did not exist in the early days of the Church (that is, the books of the New Testament were still in the process of being written and collected together). What would your Christian life have been like if you had lived then? What would have shaped and nourished your faith?

10. The Church is the place where we listen to the word of God. How true is this for me? Would my understanding of Scripture be different if I was not a member of the Church?

EIGHT

As You Continue Reading

All scripture is inspired by God and is useful for teaching, for refutation, for correction, and for training in righteousness, so that one who belongs to God may be competent, equipped for every good work.

— 2 Tim 3:16-17

The Variety of Scripture

Since the word of God is given to us as spiritual food, we shouldn't be surprised to find that it comes in as many varieties as natural food. Life would be dull indeed if all we ate was oatmeal three times a day, day after day — even specially enriched oatmeal that provided a nutritionally sound diet. Instead, we are glad to have the great variety of foods that God has given us to eat and the great variety of ways in which they can be prepared.

Scripture comes in a similar variety. The Psalms are quite different from the historical books of the Old Testament, and they in turn from the prophets. Paul's letters are quite different from the Gospels, and they in turn from the book of Revelation. They are all God's word to us, yet a word spoken in a great variety of ways. Our spiritual life would be much poorer if every book of the Bible were exactly like every other.

It is tempting to believe that if the Bible is the word of God, then every word of it must be equally holy and worthy of our attention. However, once we have made some progress in reading the Bible, we discover that some portions of it seem to have less to say to us than other portions. Some passages of Scripture don't seem to have any relevance to us, and we may even find ourselves bored as we read them. We might not admit to ourselves that we are bored, however; it would seem disrespectful to be bored by a word that God thought worth speaking to us.

It is tempting to believe that if the Bible is the word of God, then every word of it must be equally holy and worthy of our attention.

There is no use, however, pretending that we find every page of Scripture vitally interesting if we do not. Even if we can fool ourselves, we can't fool God. What is more, he might not expect us to find every verse equally important. He might be quite understanding if we admit that some passages don't hold our interest very long and seem to lack application in our lives.

I believe that our reading of Scripture should be selective, and that we should pay more attention to those passages which do have a clear message for us than to passages that seemingly lack such a message. Rather than strain to extract a message from the second set of sanctuary construction details in Exodus 36-40, or the "Oracles against the Nations" in Jeremiah 46-51, we might read such sections rather quickly and pay greater attention to the other chapters in these books.

Just as we eat various foods in order to have a balanced diet, so we need to read all the various kinds of Scripture for a balanced spiritual life.

I believe that all of Scripture is worth reading, but that some parts are more worth reading than others and should have a greater claim on our time. I also believe that we should be slow to dismiss any section of Scripture as pointless. But that isn't to say that its point will necessarily be clear to us now. And rather than get bogged down reading chapters that seem to lack meaning for us at the time, I think it is preferable to devote more attention to those chapters that more clearly speak God's word to us.

On the other hand, just as we eat various foods in order to have a balanced diet, so we need to read all the various kinds of

Scripture for a balanced spiritual life. To focus exclusively on one section of the Bible is to miss out on much that Scripture can teach us. But just as we cook or prepare different kinds of foods in different ways in order to best enhance their nutritional value and taste, so we can read different books of the Bible in different ways, in order to best draw out their meaning for us.

Some books we may have to study, particularly the first time we read them. We may have to make use of a commentary, and we might find our reading a spiritually dry experience. By contrast, our reading of more familiar books of the Bible, particularly the Gospels, can be done more simply, and we will usually have a more immediate sense of God speaking to us in a personal way. Some books of the Bible we can read more rapidly, in big chunks; other books require slow reading, with pauses for meditation. After finishing reading some books, we may find that we have learned a lot; after reading other books, we may find that we have prayed a lot.

After finishing reading some books, we may find that we have learned a lot; after reading other books, we may find that we have prayed a lot.

We might even want to experiment with reading Scripture aloud. When we learned to read in school, we were taught to read without moving our lips so that we might read faster. That is probably how we read the Bible today: silently, to ourselves. In the ancient world, however, Scripture was normally read out loud, even if a person was reading only for himself or herself. For example, the book of Acts tells of the deacon Philip going out on the road from Jerusalem to Gaza, where he sees an Ethiopian riding in a chariot and reading Scripture. "Philip ran up and heard him reading Isaiah the prophet" (Acts 8:30). Philip heard him reading Isaiah because the Ethiopian was reading out loud.

The custom of reading aloud persisted for many centuries. In his *Confessions,* written around A.D. 400, St. Augustine speaks of visiting St. Ambrose and finding him reading silently

(*Confessions,* Book 6, chapter 3). This strikes Augustine as being enough out of the ordinary that he hazards some guesses why Ambrose might be doing such a thing — an indication that reading was still normally done out loud.

Reading Scripture aloud has benefits for us today. It can help us notice things that we might miss if we read the same passage silently. Reading aloud can help a passage come alive for us by more thoroughly involving us in it. Reading out loud also forces us to read more slowly, which in turn helps us grasp its meaning.

Try not to worry about stumbling and mispronouncing words when you read aloud; you aren't trying to win an award for dramatic reading. Focus attention on the text, rather than on how you sound. You might be self-conscious the first few times you try it, but it will probably become easier for you as you do it more. (If it doesn't, then stop doing it; reading aloud should help, not be a new burden.)

Some books of the Bible are more suited for reading aloud than others — the poetic passages of the prophets more than the historical books of the Old Testament, for example. The Psalms are the best suited of all Scripture for reading aloud, since they were composed to be sung or recited.

Special Verses

In the course of our reading Scripture, we often come upon a verse or passage that has special meaning for us. We may be reading along when certain words seem to leap from the page or strike us as significant. We may have the sense that a particular verse was written with us in mind, addressing something in our lives today. In the excerpt from St. Augustine printed in Chapter Three, Augustine referred to the passage of Scripture that St. Anthony heard as God's particular word to him, and Augustine also quoted the passage that brought him to conversion. In my own life, one of the verses that has long carried particular meaning for me relates Jesus' words, "It was not you who chose me, but I who chose you and appointed you to go and bear fruit that will remain" (Jn 15:16). I apply this verse to my service as a writer. Another important verse for me, which helps me keep my writing in perspective, is "When you have done all you have been commanded, say, 'We are unprofitable servants; we have done what we were obliged to do'" (Lk 17:10).

One of the verses that has long carried particular meaning for me relates Jesus' words, "It was not you who chose me, but I who chose you and appointed you to go and bear fruit that will remain" (Jn 15:16).

We should be grateful for such special verses and pay particular attention to them. I usually mark them in the margin with pencil as I am doing my daily reading, and then return to these verses when I am done reading, to reflect on them and make them a part of my prayer that day. Reading the Bible for its overall meaning is important, but so is reading it for its particular meaning for us today. Those verses that strike us in a special way each day can convey God's word to us, as the message we need to hear and treasure that day.

There is even an advantage to memorizing these special verses as we find them. Many Christians have committed entire blocks of the Bible to memory, a feat that is beyond me. But I believe it is worthwhile to selectively memorize some verses from Scripture. The most important verses of Scripture for us to memorize will be those that have special meaning for us because they contain a very important truth or they seem to have particular application to our lives. And the easiest verses to memorize will be those that seem to speak to us directly, that seem to convey God's word addressed specifically to us.

I have always had a hard time memorizing anything, but find that there are certain Scripture verses that stick in my memory. They are lodged there because they have special meaning for me and have served as guideposts in my life. I did not make a special effort to memorize them, but I read and pondered on their meaning often enough that their words are a part of me.

They now come to mind as I am praying, or thinking, or even as I simply let my mind wander. They remind me of the truths on which I have tried to base my life.

Whatever systems of formal or informal memorization we use, the goal should be the same: to have available in our minds those verses of Scripture that are the truths we live by, so that they can spontaneously be a part of our thoughts and prayers.

One advantage of memorizing certain verses from the Bible is that we can use these verses to counter temptation. We usually battle the same old sins and weaknesses year after year, making progress on some fronts while barely holding our own on others. We need to employ all the weapons we can in our battle against our ingrained failings: prayer, unceasing effort, penance. One weapon that we can add to our arsenal is Scripture verses that address our specific faults and strengthen us against our chronic temptations. There are often Scripture verses that match up with our specific situation and speak the precise word of God we need to hear.

> Whatever systems of formal or informal memorization we use, the goal should be the same: to have available in our minds those verses of Scripture that are the truths we live by, so that they can spontaneously be a part of our thoughts and prayers.

For example, if our temptation is to sacrifice everything on the altar of our jobs, Jesus' words, "What profit would there be for one to gain the whole world and forfeit his life" or her life? (Mt 16:26), may be the message we need to reflect on. At one point in my life, when a particular Christian service was more of a burden than I wanted to bear, I often turned to a verse from 1 Peter to strengthen me: "For to this you have been called, because Christ also suffered for you, leaving you an example that you should follow in his footsteps" (1 Pet 2:21).

When You Encounter Difficulties

The Bible is both a book of life for us, and a book of a lifetime. There will be no end to the additional meaning and insight we get from it as we continue reading.

It shouldn't bewilder or discourage us, then, if there are portions of the Bible that we do not understand. Our continued reading and study will bring us greater insight, and the problem areas should gradually diminish. The Bible explains itself: our increased familiarity with Scripture will provide the context for understanding the more difficult or obscure books of Scripture. Reading books about the Bible is also an indispensable help, if we are to journey from twentieth-first-century Western patterns of thought back several thousand years to Hebrew patterns of thought and manners of expression.

Yet we shouldn't be surprised if difficulties still remain and if some passages still perplex us. The second letter of Peter makes reference to the difficulty of understanding Paul's writings (2 Pet 3:16), and if an inspired writer had difficulty understanding Paul, our own struggles should not be unexpected. Occasionally, I can finish reading a passage of Scripture only to realize I have little or no idea what it means.

And consider the patience of our Lord as salvation, as our beloved brother Paul, according to the wisdom given to him, also wrote to you, speaking of these things as he does in all his letters. In them there are some things hard to understand.

— 2 Pet 3:15-16

I've found four ways of dealing with passages I don't understand.

First of all, I remind myself that there is no merit in reading words that I don't understand. If I breeze through a passage without paying sufficient attention to what it says, I might as well not have read it. Therefore, if I find myself reading words mechanically, I stop, go back to the beginning, and reread them slowly, trying to be more attentive to their meaning. I might even have to reread a third time.

Second, I may read without understanding if I'm distracted and trying to do two things at once: read the Bible and think about something else. The cure for this is to put distractions and preoccupations out of my mind as much as possible and resolve not to be doing anything but reading Scripture during my Scripture reading.

Third, a difficult passage may make more sense in a different translation. I sometimes reread a passage in a second or third translation if I am baffled by what it means. This doesn't always help (some passages are obscure in every translation), but it quite often throws a fresh light on a perplexing passage.

Even on difficult days, we should read anyway. Just because one day's reading does not seem to have an immediate effect on us does not mean that our reading has been in vain.

Fourth, I have bought a number of commentaries on the books of the Bible through the years, allowing me to read what scholars have to say about passages I find obscure. Usually, I find an explanation that I can understand and that satisfies me. But if scholars suggest interpretations that I find unconvincing, I will often prefer to remain puzzled.

If angels read Scripture, they probably read it with rapt attention every day, instantly understanding its meaning and lifting their whole beings to God in prayer. But since they already see God face-to-face, they don't need to make use of the intermediary of his word in the Bible.

Those of us who are not angels, however, will probably not read the Bible with an equal sense of fulfillment every day. There are days when God seems to speak directly to us through the words of Scripture, when our minds are filled with insight and awe, when our hearts are deeply touched by God's presence. And there are days when none of these things seem to happen, and we think we might as well have been reading the classified ad section of the newspaper for all the good our reading apparently did us. These days may come more often when we are reading some of the more obscure books of the Old Testament.

Even on difficult days, we should read anyway. Just because one day's reading does not seem to have an immediate effect on us does not mean that our reading has been in vain. Even the least rewarding books of the Bible convey something of God's revelation to us and prepare us to better understand the rest of Scripture.

Scripture reading is like marriage: there are days when the duties of marriage and family life outweigh the thrill, but they are a part of marriage and form the background for those times when husband and wife do experience the deep blessings of having been given to each other. The joys of marriage are based on the faithfulness, come what may, of husband and wife to each other. So, too, our Scripture reading: the blessings we receive depend on our faithfulness.

We are sure to find obscure passages when we read the Bible, things that won't make sense to us without some kind of help. The ceremony described in Genesis 15, whereby God sealed a covenant with Abraham, must strike us as odd, until we discover that this was the way contracts were solemnized in the days before notary publics. On the other hand, the first four verses of chapter six of Genesis may continue to be obscure for us even after we have studied them, and to seemingly lack any implications for our lives today.

When we encounter such perplexities, we need to keep in mind that we read the Bible for what we can understand of it, not for what we cannot understand. Puzzling over difficulties should not occupy most of our time or attention; we should focus on what we do understand and peacefully consign what we don't understand to a corner of our minds. We shouldn't let obscurities distract us from God speaking to us through what we do understand.

Small-Group Sharing

Jesus addresses us as individuals when we read his word in Scripture. His word is a personal word to us, a message that is no less personal for also being a message to others. But Jesus also wants to address his word to us as his followers gathered together in his name. He wants to speak his word to us not only through the words of the Bible as we read them but through one another's words as we share what Scripture means to us.

> He wants to speak his word to us not only through the words of the Bible as we read them but through one another's words as we share what Scripture means to us.

Jesus promised, "Where two or three are gathered together in my name, there am I in the midst of them" (Mt 18:20). Jesus is present when we share our lives as Christians with one another. When we tell others how we have heard the word of God addressed to us, we help them hear the word that is spoken to them.

A Bible-sharing group can be set up quite simply. As few as four people who meet regularly can make up a successful Scripture-sharing group, although six to eight is a better number. The faithfulness of people's attendance and the openness with which they share are more important than striving for any particular number. Most groups find that weekly meetings work best, although some groups set their meetings for every two weeks.

Different meeting formats can be used to provide a framework for sharing. It is usually best to have one person designated as the leader of the meeting. This might be a different person each week, or one person might be the leader for an extended period of time. The meeting should begin and end with prayer. Many groups make these times opportunities for informal shared prayer, with each person feeling free to pray aloud in their own words. If a group isn't comfortable with this style of prayer, the leader should lead the group in a form of prayer that they can enter into wholeheartedly.

In a Scripture sharing group, the leader does not have to function as an expert, able to answer everyone's questions about the Bible. Rather, the role of the leader is to help the members of the group share with one another, keeping the discussion focused on the Bible. This might mean encouraging the quieter members to share more and the more vocal members to listen more (to be done tactfully!). Or it might mean bringing the group back to the words of Scripture if the discussion goes too far afield. Once in a while, the leader might have to end a line of discussion and begin a new one.

> The role of the leader is to help the members of the group share with each other, keeping the discussion focused on the Bible.

The main attention of a Scripture-sharing group should be on the words of Scripture as they speak to the lives of the participants of the group. The meeting should not be a discussion about Scripture in the abstract; it should be a sharing of what Scripture means in the life of each member of the group. Although it can be helpful for a member of the group to say something about the historical background of a Scripture passage in order that everyone might understand it better, or share something he or she read about a passage that helped them understand its meaning, the focus of the group should be on personal discussion of their Christian lives as addressed by the word of God.

> The focus of the group should be on personal discussion of their Christian lives as addressed by the word of God.

Some groups share thoughts about a common passage that they have all read; other groups base their sharing on whatever Scripture each member has read in the past week. If the discussion is to be about one passage, it is best to have that passage read aloud by one member of the group and then pause for a time of silent reflection and listening. Sometimes, reading the passage aloud a second or third time later in the meeting will provide an opportunity for hearing God speak more strongly and spark a new depth of discussion.

After the passage has been read and there have been a few moments of silent reflection, the leader can initiate the sharing by asking open-ended questions:

- What was the author of this passage of Scripture trying to convey to the reader at that time?
- How do you understand these words to apply to your life?
- Does anyone think that God is addressing these words to them in a particular way?

It should be expected that a group will grow in its ability to share as its members grow to know and love one another. A group that might start with rather restrained sharing and occasional awkward silences may soon find that discussion flows freely and the meeting time passes quickly.

Meetings should initially be scheduled to last about an hour and a half, and then later tailored to the group's needs and interests. It is often desirable to have light refreshments at the end, so that purely social sharing can be held off until that time. It is better to have a shorter set time for Scripture sharing, and adhere to that time limit, than to have a long or indefinite meeting time that allows wandering off onto other topics.

There is also a second type of small group Scripture meeting, a Bible study group. In contrast to a sharing group, where the aim is to share what the Bible means for our lives, the aim of a study group is to learn more about the Bible itself. A study group needs more resources to be successful.

The ideal leader for a study group is someone who can teach the group and answer questions. If such a person isn't available, then the group could listen to (or watch) a series of tapes, CDs, or DVDs and discuss them; make use of one of the packaged programs of Scripture study available today; or read and discuss some book about the Bible, treating it as a textbook. While study groups do require more resources and work than sharing groups, they also give their members a greater depth of understanding of Scripture and lay the groundwork for better sharing of Scripture.

Year after Year

Presumably, age should bring wisdom along with gray hair. What have I learned about reading the Bible after having doing it for many years? There are a few things I might say.

I began to read Scripture on Ash Wednesday, 1964. I had dipped into the Bible before but never read it in a serious or sustained way. As a result of making a Cursillo (a weekend "short course in Christianity"), I resolved to read Scripture every day during Lent. It was a modest enough commitment: fifteen minutes of Scripture reading and reflection after my breakfast coffee had taken effect. When Lent was over, I kept on reading. And by the grace of God, I read Scripture to hear God's word to me and to respond to him in prayer.

My aim is to open myself to God's word whenever I read the Bible or hear its words proclaimed.

I realize now what a great grace from God this was, getting me off on the right foot. I still try to read Scripture or listen to it proclaimed in the Liturgy in the same way I did when I began: as God's word to me. This doesn't mean I always succeed (distractions are ever-beckoning fields in which my mind is eager to frolic), but my aim is to open myself to God's word whenever I read the Bible or hear its words proclaimed.

I don't want to downplay the importance of studying the Bible and making use of the work of scholars. Much of my time over the last decades was spent studying the Bible in order to write about it. This involved consulting commentaries and even wrestling in a limited way with the original Hebrew and Greek texts. But when I finished my homework with the commentaries,

I set them aside and said to myself, "Okay — granted all that the scholars say — what does this text of Scripture mean as God's word to me?"

My reflecting on Scripture is less programmed than when I first began. Initially, I had a fixed time each day for reading and reflecting, and that was my chief encounter with Scripture for the day. Now I find myself pondering the words of Scripture periodically throughout the day. One of the Scripture readings during morning Mass may trigger reflections that continue after Mass is over. A phrase or line from a hymn may echo a verse of Scripture, drawing my mind to the passage. A situation I encounter during the day may bring a scriptural parallel to mind — or a particular passage will just pop into my mind unexpectedly, bearing a meaning or application that I had never before noted. Some of this began to happen rather soon after I began regular Scripture reading, but it has become an even more common experience for me in recent years.

I don't want to give the impression that my mind is constantly taken up with God or Scripture, for it surely is not. But the cumulative effect of years of reading Scripture is that a good deal of biblical material has entered my memory banks, and it periodically pushes its way into my consciousness, drawing my mind to God.

Another byproduct of years of Scripture reading is that I know more of the context of particular biblical passages. For example, if a selection from one of the prophets is read during Mass, I often can recall the historical setting in which that prophecy was uttered. This helps me appreciate something of the significance the prophecy had for those to whom it was first addressed, and this in turn often suggests an application of the prophetic message for today. Because of my years of reading the Bible, I am now better able to understand Scripture contextually — a dimension of its meaning I often missed when I first began to read the Bible.

My first years of reading Scripture were filled with the excitement of new discovery. I had never encountered most of the books of the Bible, much less taken their words to heart. When I began to read the Bible, I had the expectation that I would discover something new and transforming every day. By the grace of the Holy Spirit, I usually did.

Through the years, much of that excitement has worn off, but not the sense of newness. I am amazed that I still discover new insights each time I read the Gospels, even though I have read them many times through the years and studied them with the help of a fair number of commentaries. The Bible is no longer new to me in the sense of novelty but new in the sense of always containing new depths of meaning that await my discovery.

The ever-newness of Scripture is partly a characteristic of Scripture and partly a grace God gives us as we read it. St. Augustine noted that no matter how long and diligently he studied the Bible, he would always find new treasures of meaning in it every day. I think God gives most everyone who perseveres in reading Scripture over a number of years a sense of what Augustine describes.

> For such is the depth of the Christian Scriptures, that even if I were attempting to study them and nothing else, from early boyhood to decrepit old age, with the utmost leisure, the most unwearied zeal, and talents greater than I have, I would still be daily making progress in discovering their treasures.
>
> — St. Augustine, *Letter* 137, written in A.D. 412

If I don't always find reading Scripture as exciting as I remember it being decades ago, neither is my marriage as exciting as it was in the days when my wife Mary and I faced life with the energy and idealism of newlyweds. But that does not mean that our marriage has gone downhill. To the contrary: our love has deepened and matured through the years. I now love and appreciate Mary far more than I did when we were first married.

Growth in marriage is a good analogy for growth in reading Scripture, for both are a matter of a relationship. Reading Scripture is a facet of our relationship with God and cannot be understood apart from it. Has my relationship with God changed through the years? Of course. So it should be no surprise that my reading of the Bible as his word has changed as well.

Growth in reading Scripture should be growth in our understanding of its inspired meaning but also growth in taking it to heart. I know I have grown in my understanding of the books of the Bible; growth in taking it to heart is harder to measure. The difficulty is one of measuring growth in our relationship with God. Feeling holier doesn't necessarily mean being holier: the Pharisee praying in the temple in Jesus' parable certainly felt holy (see Lk 18:9-14).

Spiritual writers warn that as we grow closer to God, our prayers may become dry and unrewarding, and so, too, our reading of Scripture. The voice of God may seem to grow silent as God trains us to hear him more accurately.

The great spiritual writers of the Church have insisted that growth in holiness is not a matter of achieving ever higher spiritual highs. So, too, growth in reading Scripture cannot be a matter of attaining ever greater ecstasies as we read. If God chooses to motivate us by such means, fine; but they aren't the reason we read his word, and their absence does not mean that he is no longer speaking to us. Spiritual writers warn that as we grow closer to God, our prayers may become dry and unrewarding, and so, too, our reading of Scripture. The voice of God may seem to grow silent as God trains us to hear him more accurately. But just as it is important to persevere in prayer even when it is unrewarding, so we must persevere in reading Scripture even when its words no longer move us as they once did. We are seeking the one behind the words, and ultimately our quest becomes wordless.

I hope these reflections encourage you to stick with reading Scripture, in season and out of season, whether you think you're treading water or making progress. Don't expect that God will speak to you the same way through Scripture today as he did five, or ten, or twenty-five or fifty years ago. Learn as much about the Bible as you can, and then go before God, alone with his word, and listen to what he has to say to you. Don't demand he speak with thunder and lightning when he is trying to talk to you in a still small voice. Don't mistake his silence for his not speaking. Don't stop reading; don't stop listening. Abide in his word, as in a marriage that will never end.

I pray that God will give me the grace to do just that: abide in his word, until in eternity he speaks to me face-to-face.

Resources

The pioneering Catholic small group Scripture study program is the *Little Rock Scripture Study*, a ministry of the Little Rock diocese in partnership with the Liturgical Press. Materials are available through the Liturgical Press, and information is posted at http://www.littlerockscripture.org.

Two other excellent small group Scripture study and sharing programs are the *Six Weeks With The Bible* series, written/edited by Kevin Perrotta and published by Loyola Press (www.loyolapress.com), and the *Threshold Bible Study* series by Stephen J. Binz, published by Twenty-Third Publications (www.twentythirdpublications.com).

Study Guide

1. Have I come across sections of the Bible that puzzled me? bored me? angered me? What are my favorite sections of the Bible? my least favorite? What parts of the Bible am I least familiar with? What is the best balance for me between drawing nourishment from the portions of the Bible I find most nourishing and yet not completely neglecting the portions I find difficult to understand and apply?

2. Have I ever read the Bible out loud to myself? Was it helpful or unhelpful for me to do so? Suggestion: Select a psalm and read it aloud as a part of your prayers today.

3. Are there particular biblical verses that have special meaning for me? What are these verses? How did I first come across them? What gives them their special meaning for me?

4. Do I find memorizing easy or difficult? Are there passages of Scripture that I can repeat from memory? How has having these passages readily at hand been of help to me? Do I have other favorite biblical passages that would be helpful to memorize?

5. The second letter of Peter says that in Paul's letters "there are some things hard to understand" (2 Pet 3:16). Should I be surprised if there are portions of the Bible I have trouble understanding, or if there are questions about the Bible I cannot answer?

6. If I find myself reading a Scripture passage I don't understand, how do I react? What do I do? How well does it work?

7. We read the Bible for what we can understand of it, not for what we cannot understand. Do I let perplexities distract me from the meaning I can understand? Do I let uncertainties excuse me from putting into practice what is certain?

8. Am I, or have I been, a part of a Bible study or sharing group, or other small sharing group? How has being a member of the group benefited me? What do I like about group sharing? What do I find difficult?

9. If I am not part of a Bible-sharing group, how might being in such a group be of help to me in reading, understanding, and applying the words of Scripture? Is there a group I could join? Could I form a new group with some of my friends?

Conclusion

*And now I commend you to God and to that gracious word
of his that can build you up and give you the inheritance
among all who are consecrated.*

— ACTS 20:32

Of all cities in which Paul proclaimed the good news of Jesus,
none received more of Paul's attention than Ephesus. Ephesus was the capital of the Roman province of Asia; its site lies on
the western Mediterranean coast of modern Turkey. Paul stayed
in Ephesus for three years (Acts 20:31), longer than in any other
city during his missionary journeys.

After his extended stay in Ephesus, Paul spent some months
in Greece, and then sailed back toward Ephesus. Paul was anxious to get to Jerusalem in time to celebrate Pentecost, and so did
not go into Ephesus itself (Acts 20:16). Instead he stopped at the
nearby seaport town of Miletus and sent for the leaders of the
Church at Ephesus to visit him there. They were his dear friends,
his converts, his co-workers, and he wanted to say goodbye to
them before continuing on to Jerusalem.

Paul's farewell was an especially heartfelt one. The Holy
Spirit had revealed that persecution and imprisonment lay before him (Acts 20:23). Paul told his Ephesian friends, "But now I
know that none of you to whom I preached the kingdom during
my travels will ever see my face again" (Acts 20:25). Paul spoke
words of farewell to them, and then:

> . . . when he had finished speaking he knelt down and
> prayed with them all. They were all weeping loudly as

they threw their arms around Paul and kissed him, for
they were deeply distressed that he had said that they
would never see his face again. Then they escorted him
to the ship.

— ACTS 20:36-38

This setting gives Paul's final exhortation to the Ephesians
special significance. Paul was not merely giving out good general
advice; Paul was addressing last words of instruction to
close friends who were responsible for guiding the Church at
Ephesus. The moment was a solemn one, not to be wasted.

Paul exhorted the leaders to watch over the Church at Ephesus
with diligence, reminding them of his own example. And
then he gave them a final solemn word of exhortation and encouragement:

And now I commend you to God and to that gracious
word of his that can build you up and give you the inheritance
among all who are consecrated.

— ACTS 20:32

The "gracious word" that Paul referred to was the message
of salvation that he had handed on to them, the message that
was even then being put into writing as the books of the New
Testament. The gracious word was the good news of who Jesus
Christ is and what he has done for us. The gracious word was the
message through which we, too, find salvation.

If Paul were to address a farewell message to us, it would
likely be the same message. He would commend us into the
hands of God, reminding us of the loving care the Father has
for us. He would remind us that true life comes to us through
Jesus Christ, God's provision for our eternal salvation. He would
exhort us to be filled with the Holy Spirit and to live out our
lives as sons and daughters of God. And Paul would exhort us
to draw daily strength from the message of salvation that we

have heard, from the good news that has been handed on to us, from the word of God that has been addressed to us. He would remind us that the word of God in Scripture is a word of grace and power that can build us up.

Our part must be to be faithful to the word of God — faithful in reading it in Scripture, faithful in embracing it. God will be faithful to us, speaking to us, drawing us to himself.

Sources Quoted in This Book
(LISTED CHRONOLOGICALLY)

St. Ephrem the Syrian:

Quotation from the *Commentary on the Diatessaron* attributed to St. Ephrem is found in *Biblical Interpretation* by Joseph W. Trigg (Wilmington, DE: Michael Glazier, 1988), p. 38.

St. Augustine:

Quotation from Book VIII, Chapter 12 of the *Confessions* is taken from The *Confessions of St. Augustine* translated by Rex Warner (New York: New American Library, 1963), pp. 182-183.

Quotation from *Letter 137* is taken from *The Nicene and Post-Nicene Fathers, First Series, Vol. 1* (Grand Rapids: Eerdmans, 1983), p. 474.

St. Teresa of Ávila:

Quotation from Chapter 8 of her Life is taken from *Conversation with Christ* by Peter-Thomas Rohrbach, O.C.D. (Notre Dame, IN: Fides, 1956), p. 3.

The Second Vatican Council:

Quotations in this book from the documents of the Second Vatican Council are from the English translations posted on the Vatican's Web site.

The *Dogmatic Constitution on the Church* is posted at http://www.vatican.va/archive/hist_councils/ii_vatican_council/documents/vat-ii_const_19641121_lumen-gentium_en.html.

The *Dogmatic Constitution on Divine Revelation* is posted at http://www.vatican.va/archive/hist_councils/ii_vatican_council/documents/vat-ii_const_19651118_dei-verbum_en.html.

The documents of the Second Vatican Council are also available in a translation by Austin P. Flannery, O.P.: *The Documents of Vatican II* (New York: Costello Publishing Company, 1975).

Pope John Paul II:

His address of April 23, 1993, on The Interpretation of the Bible in the Church was given in French and published in English translation in *L'Osservatore Romano* on April 28, 1993, and reprinted in the Vatican edition of The Pontifical Biblical Commission's document, *The Interpretation of the Bible in the Church* (Vatican City: Libreria Editrice Vaticana, 1993). The quotation in Chapter Three of this book is found on page 15 of this edition, and the quotation in Chapter Six of this book is found on page 17.

The address is posted on the Vatican Web site (in Italian and Portuguese translations) at http://www.vatican.va/roman_curia/congregations/cfaith/pcb_index.htm.

Pope Benedict XVI:

The quotation in Chapter Four of this book is taken from Pope Benedict XVI's Message to the Youth of the World on the Occasion of the 21st World Youth Day, April 9, 2006.

The text of this message is posted at http://www.vatican.va/holy_father/benedict_xvi/messages/youth/documents/hf_ben-xvi_mes_20060222_youth_en.html.